W9-AHL-961

Volpone, or the Fox

Crofts Classics

GENERAL EDITORS

Samuel H. Beer, *Harvard University*

O. B. Hardison, Jr., *The Folger Shakespeare Library*

BEN JONSON

Volpone, or the Fox

EDITED BY

Jonas A. Barish

UNIVERSITY OF CALIFORNIA, BERKELEY

AHM Publishing Corporation
Arlington Heights, Illinois 60004

Copyright © 1958
AHM PUBLISHING CORPORATION

All rights reserved

This book, or parts thereof, must not be used
or reproduced in any manner, without written
permission. For information address the pub-
lisher, AHM PUBLISHING CORPORATION,
3110 North Arlington Heights Road, Arlington
Heights, Illinois 60004.

ISBN: 0-88295-049-5
(Formerly 0-390-22704-8)

Library of Congress Card Number: 58-6112

PRINTED IN THE UNITED STATES OF AMERICA
778
Seventeenth Printing

INTRODUCTION

By one of those ironies that have dogged Ben Jonson's reputation ever since the Shakespeare idolatry of the modern era got underway, tributes to Jonson's learning have somehow been converted into stigmas on his artistry. The fact that he was a scholar, known for his habit of paraphrasing from the Greek and Latin classics in his plays, has obscured the fact that he was primarily an inventive man of the theater. But if we look coolly at his achievement, we discover that despite his erudition and his readiness to tap literary tradition, he experimented more boldly with new forms of drama than any of his contemporaries. To be sure, not all of his experiments succeeded. But in those that did —*Volpone,* for example—Jonson created a kind of comedy unique in the theater of the world.

Jonson arrived on the literary scene, at the end of the sixteenth century, at a moment when the prevailing mode of comedy was "romantic." Romantic comedy invited audiences to suspend their workaday preoccupations and immerse themselves in a world of magic and revelry where probability was flouted at every turn, where dukes consorted with milkmaids and princes in disguise wooed shepherdesses, where mortals in distress received miraculous aid from fairies and goddesses, where marvellous reunions took place between parents and long-lost children, where young lovers recited rhapsodic love poetry to each other, and where interludes of clowning, music, and pageantry might interrupt the progress of the story at any moment.

Against this kind of comedy Jonson objected that it trampled on every principle of art. Instead of imitating life, it retreated into escapist fantasies; instead of creating recognizable human characters, it preferred to imagine monsters and goblins. It made only the most half-hearted attempts to weld its diverse elements into coherent artistic structures. Above all, in Jonson's eye, and at the root of its other defects, it aimed only to amuse, and so surrendered the artist's traditional responsibility of inculcating virtue. It sent its spectators home pleased with themselves instead of newly awakened to a knowledge of their own follies.

For his own part, Jonson, in revolt against what he considered an unnatural set of conventions, set out single-handed to reform English comedy. Armed with the famous definition, attributed to Cicero, of comedy as *imitatio vitae, speculum consuetudinis, imago veritatis*—the imitation of life, the mirror of custom, the image of truth—he interpreted this to mean that the theater should deal with the familiar rather than the remote, that it should banish marvels and improbabilities from its plots, in short, that it should aim at a realistic portrayal of life. In pursuit of this aim he chose for his own setting not the greenwood of pastoral comedy or the mythical kingdoms of Arcadia or Illyria, but the shops and street-corners of the city, and he peopled this scene not with disguised princes and ship-wrecked princesses, but with the ordinary citizens who actually inhabited it: rich merchants, penniless knights, idle law-students, clerks, apprentices, and tavern-keepers. In place of the high-flown lyricism of the romantic drama, he bestowed on his characters an idiom compounded from the colloquial speech of the marketplace. For the familiar intrigue plot, with its cross-wooings and strange adventures and rambling structure, he evolved a plot of his own, designed to exhibit the kinds of folly one met among one's neighbors, and he fiercely excluded from it the pageantry with which romantic drama had fed the public taste for spectacle.

If Cicero provided him with a working definition of comedy, the Roman comic playwrights Plautus and Terence supplied him with a formula for character that he could develop in accordance with Elizabethan popular psychology. Such stock figures of Latin comedy as the scheming parasite, the braggart soldier, the spendthrift heir, each with a fixed personality determined by his age, sex, social rank, and occupation, became transmuted in Jonson's hands into a gallery of eccentrics, each pursuing to the exclusion of everything else in the world his own eccentricity, or humor, so named from the four humors, or body fluids, the balance or imbalance among which was believed to govern temperament. A man ridden by an aberration was said to be "in his humor"—hence the title of Jonson's first experimental play, *Every Man in His Humor*, in which characters like the jealous husband, the boastful coward, the anxious father, partly modelled on their Latin prototypes, showed how insidiously the dominant humor could tyrannize over a man's disposition. On the other hand, many of the so-called humors, in Jonson's view, were not genuine physiological disturbances at all, but mere affectations, idle pretentiousness on the part of nonentities wishing to appear fashionably "interesting." Affectation, as it was only skin-deep, might be cured: a man could be shaken "out of his humor" by being made to see his folly clearly—hence the title of Jonson's next experiment, *Every Man out of His Humor*, which concentrated on ingenious stratagems of ridicule by which affected characters are jolted out of their foolishness and back to sanity.

By conceiving of personality as fixed and obsessive, Jonson was able to populate a whole stage full of characters compulsively acting out their private fantasies, in whom the spectators could see their own quirks magnified to grotesque proportions, laugh at them, and—presumably—mend them. The problem was to devise a plot that would exhibit such follies without sacrificing momentum or cohesion. In Jonson's early plays the action tends to reduce itself to a series of brilliant sketches; even the sketches sometimes buckle under the strain of having been contrived solely as a vehicle for the display of eccentricity. But with his tragedy *Sejanus*, Jonson hit upon the device of the conspiracy as a lever for prying open the recesses of human viciousness, and with *Volpone*, he triumphantly turned the same theme to comic purposes. The conspiracy, by showing men grasping criminally after the satisfaction of their appetites, probes something far more deep-seated and malevolent in human nature than mere eccentricity. At the same time, it involves purpose and conflict, and so propels action forward strongly.

Volpone, the first of Jonson's major comic masterpieces, had its initial performances at the Globe Theatre in 1606. Nothing like it had ever been seen before on the English stage, and—one may add—nothing like it has been seen since. Drawing freely on the vast literature of folly that had been accumulating since Aristophanes, Jonson achieved a play that was at once a monument of eclecticism and a a tower of originality. As the mainspring of his plot and his chief symbol of dehumanized greed, he transferred into the Italian Renaissance the ancient Roman practice of legacy-hunting, described by the satirists of the early empire. Several vivid little sketches by the late Greek rhetorician

Lucian, and the famous mock-eulogy of folly by the Renaissance humanist Erasmus, provided him with enriching detail for his own vision of human absurdity.

For his scene Jonson turned to Venice, a symbol of worldly splendor, and also of the violent passions and Machiavellian intrigue regarded by Renaissance Englishmen as typically Italian. For his *dramatis personae*, he chose not the simple eccentrics of his earlier comedy, but an array of frightening monomaniacs, devoured by avarice and ready to use any means to satisfy it. By naming them after animals, in the manner of the ancient beast-fable, he underscored their resemblance to the beasts for which they were named, and hence the unnaturalness of their behavior. The plot, converting the antique game of legacy-hunting into a Venetian swindle, artfully complicates the swindle by making the legacy-hunters the victims of their own prey, and the prey itself, the supposedly dying Volpone, leagued with his resourceful parasite Mosca, the perpetrator of a hoax that grows steadily more intricate until it finally flies apart like a time-bomb from its own inner pressure. And as a warning, perhaps, to his own countrymen, he placed alongside the predatory Venetians the blundering English travellers Sir Politic and Lady Wouldbe, shrilly trying to parrot the Venetians in all the worst ways. Sir Politic and Lady Wouldbe, survivors from Jonson's earlier comedy of humors, suffer from affectation rather than perversion. Their rather frantic efforts to mimic Italian cunning lead, therefore, to scenes of exposure in which they cover themselves with ridicule, confront their own folly, and presumably are purged of it.

Like Jonson's earlier comedy, *Volpone* has a moral purpose, but it effects its moral more through negative example than through direct exhortation. The opening scene, in which Volpone blasphemously adores his gold, plunges us at once into a world where moral values are inverted, and the subsequent scenes, in which he feigns sick, develop a stage metaphor in which his counterfeit physical illness comes to stand for his actual spiritual disease. The trio of deformed pets who caper around the household offer repellent visual testimony to the unnaturalness of this diseased world, but they form a spectacle less ridiculous and terrifying than that of the three birds of prey, Voltore, Corbaccio, and Corvino, who hover near the bedside scenting carrion. Each of Volpone's masquerades carries within it the terms of its own hollowness. The fraudulent elixir that he advertises with his gaudy mountebank's rhetoric proves to be a double sham—not only in itself, but because Volpone uses it only as a device for approaching Celia—and the same is true of the bizarre splendors with which he tempts Celia herself. To effect a common seduction he conjures up a voluptuary's paradise as dazzling and as illusory as the magic cures promised by the elixir.

But it is characteristic of Volpone to embroider his meanest acts with the gilt of his rhetoric. He does so with such zest and spellbinding power as to suggest that he himself lives half-bewitched in the world of his imagination, a captive of his own eloquence. The same uninhibited power of fantasy that insures his momentary successes against his dupes also insures his ultimate self-exposure. The overwrought imagination that can hypnotize others must end by hypnotizing itself. He and Mosca, with their superior cunning and their gusto in knavery, can perform their prodigies of deceit, hoodwinking their clients and the judicial officers at the same time, only up to the point at which, intoxicated by success, they grow reckless, turn on each other, and undo themselves.

And that point, Jonson assures us, is bound to be reached. The double doublecross of the finale instructs us that even such supreme devilry as theirs will ultimately overreach itself. The instruments of justice may be helpless to arrive at the truth, but the nature of roguery is such that at length it unmasks itself through its own excesses, exposing itself as merely another species of the folly that grows on every acre of the human landscape.

The harshness of the final sentence may make us wince a little, and even Jonson felt it necessary to defend himself against the charge of having violated the comic spirit, but *Volpone* has dealt with evil so luridly that only a ceremonial cleansing of the infected atmosphere can begin to restore our trust in the power of good. If it is fitting that Volpone and Mosca should scourge their own victims in the mock-death scene of Act V and the street scenes that follow, it is equally fitting that they should finally suffer the severest sentence of all. The well-known stringency of Venetian justice becomes a necessary counterweight to the forces of evil that have been unleashed in the course of the action.

If *Volpone* leaves us with any single final impression, it is likely to be that of the immense potentiality in men for self-perversion, for forsaking their humanity and imitating beasts, and so turning themselves into monsters, abandoning their natural affections in order to gratify their most negative instincts of envy, lust, hatred, and cunning, with a thoroughness that inhibits the pitying tears of tragedy altogether and arouses only the scornful laughter of satire. If we reserve most of our scorn for the three birds of prey, if we laugh *at* them and *with* Volpone and Mosca during most of the action, it is not only because Corvino, Voltore, and Corbaccio are so repellent, but because Volpone and Mosca act out with such marvellous aplomb our own secret craving to dominate and manipulate others. We really want to see them get away with it, but Jonson will not indulge us that far. When, in the final scene, we find ourselves laughing somewhat uneasily, it is because this time we are laughing at ourselves, seeing our own uncontrolled fantasies of wealth and power brought sternly back to earth and checked by the rigors of public morality. The wish-fulfillment of the comic world, which usually lasts right up to the final curtain, is here rudely dispelled, leaving us in no doubt that the dream has been a nightmare all along.

From the time of its first performances, *Volpone* held the stage almost without interruption down to the end of the eighteenth century, when the romantic revolution dealt it a blow from which it is still recovering. In the past generation it has been revived occasionally, and with success, but it continues in the theater largely through such adaptations as that of Stefan Zweig and Jules Romains. It is a stroke of irony that would doubtless have stung Jonson to fury that his massive onslaught on fraud should itself survive in a counterfeit version, and that a play which exposes greed as the ugliest of the passions should reach the public in a diluted form because of the venality of the box-office. But as *King Lear* freed itself from the improvements of Nahum Tate, there is no reason to doubt that *Volpone* will disengage itself in time from the officious assistance of its adaptors. When satire that cuts to the bone becomes bearable again, when audiences cease to demand "sympathetic" characters with whom to identify themselves, when they have discovered the power in Jonson's taut blank verse and the ordered elegance of his plotting, *Volpone* will be welcomed back into the theater as one of the half-dozen or so great comedies of the English language.

PRINCIPAL DATES IN JONSON'S LIFE

❧

1572 Jonson born, in or near London.

c. 1583-89 Attends Westminster School, London.

c. 1589 Apprenticed as a brick-layer to his step-father.

c. 1594 Serves in the Netherlands in the campaign against Spain.

c. 1595 Marries.

c. 1597 Enters the theater as actor and playwright in the service of the manager Philip Henslowe.

1597 Imprisoned for his share in a lost satiric comedy, *The Isle of Dogs.*

1598 *Every Man in His Humor* played by the Lord Chamberlain's Company, with Shakespeare in a leading role. Jonson duels with a fellow actor, kills him, is cited for felonious assault, and released with the felon's brand on his thumb.

1599-1601 *Every Man out of His Humor, Cynthia's Revels,* and *Poetaster,* experimental plays labelled "comical satires" by Jonson, acted in public and private playhouses. *Poetaster* caricatures two of Jonson's fellow playwrights, Dekker and Marston, who retaliate by lampooning Jonson in their own play *Satiromastix.*

1603 James I ascends the throne of England. Jonson composes a series of entertainments for the reception of the new king. *Sejanus,* Jonson's tragedy of Roman decadence, played at the Globe Theatre, leading to Jonson's arrest on suspicion of treason.

1605 Jonson voluntarily joins his two collaborators, Chapman and Marston, in prison for his share in a comedy, *Eastward Ho,* found offensive because of its satire against the Scots.

1605-25 Period of the great court masques and entertainments composed by Jonson for court festivals.

1606 *Volpone* acted at the Globe Theatre and at the two universities. Jonson and his wife, Roman Catholics at this time, summoned before the authorities for failure to take communion in the Church of England.

1609   *Epicoene, or The Silent Woman* performed by the Children of the Queen's Revels.

1612-13   Jonson travels on the continent as tutor to the son of Sir Walter Raleigh.

1614   *Bartholomew Fair* played at the Hope Theatre.

1616   Jonson publishes his collected plays in a single folio volume entitled *The Works of Benjamin Jonson*, the first such collection in the history of English bookmaking.

1616-32   Jonson's later plays, *The Devil is an Ass, The Staple of News, The New Inn,* and *The Magnetic Lady*, acted at irregular intervals with increasing lack of success.

1618   Jonson tours Scotland on foot, visiting the Scottish poet Drummond of Hawthorneden, who keeps a record of their conversations.

1623   Jonson's library, containing unpublished poems and works of scholarship, destroyed by fire. Jonson contributes commendatory verses to the first folio collection of Shakespeare's plays.

1625   Charles I ascends the throne.

1625-32   Period of the later masques and entertainments under the new monarchs, and in circumstances of bitter rivalry with the court architect and stage-designer, Inigo Jones.

1628   Jonson suffers a paralytic stroke, and spends the rest of his life as a semi-invalid, visited by a coterie of younger admirers and disciples, "The Sons of Ben."

1637   Jonson dies on August 6th. Buried in Westminster Abbey under the inscription "O Rare Ben Jonson."

BEN JONSON

Volpone, or the Fox

GREAT CHAIN OF BEING
(REASON U.S. WILL)

GOD   → BEING

ANGELS   → REASON

MAN   → REASON + WILL

ANIMALS   → SENSES, MOBILITY MEMORY

PLANTS   — FEED THEMSELVES

INANIMATE — → EXIST

VOLPONE, OR THE FOX

❧

THE PERSONS OF THE PLAY

VOLPONE, *a magnifico* FOX
MOSCA, *his parasite* FLY
VOLTORE, *an advocate* VULTURE
CORBACCIO, *an old gentleman* RAVEN
CORVINO, *a merchant* CROW
BONARIO [*son to* CORBACCIO]
SIR POLITIC WOULDBE [*a foolish knight*]
PEREGRINE, *a gentleman traveller* FALCON
NANO, *a dwarf*
CASTRONE, *an eunuch*
ANDROGYNO, *an hermaphrodite*
GREGE, *or mob*
COMMENDATORI, *officers of justice*
MERCATORI, *three merchants*
AVOCATORI, *four magistrates*
NOTARIO, *the register*

LADY WOULDBE, SIR POLITIC'S *wife*
CELIA, CORVINO'S *wife*
Servitori, Women, &c.

The Scene: VENICE

THE ARGUMENT

V OLPONE, childless, rich, feigns sick, despairs,
O ffers his state to hopes of several heirs,
L ies languishing. His parasite receives
P resents of all, assures, deludes, then weaves
O ther cross-plots, which ope themselves, are told.
N ew tricks for safety are sought; they thrive; when, bold,
E ach tempts th' other again, and all are sold.

1

PROLOGUE

Now luck yet send us, and a little wit
    Will serve to make our play hit;
According to the palates of the season,
    Here is rhyme not empty of reason.
This we were bid to credit from our poet,
    Whose true scope, if you would know it,
In all his poems still hath been this measure,
    To mix profit with your pleasure;
And not as some, whose throats their envy failing,
10   Cry hoarsely, all he writes is railing;
And when his plays come forth, think they can flout them
    With saying he was a year about them.
To these there needs no lie but this his creature,
    Which was two months since no feature.
And though he dares give them five lives to mend it,
    'Tis known, five weeks fully penned it,
From his own hand, without a coadjutor,
    Novice, journeyman, or tutor.
Yet thus much I can give you as a token
20   Of his play's worth: no eggs are broken,
Nor quaking custards with fierce teeth affrighted,
    Wherewith your rout are so delighted;
Nor hales he in a gull, old ends reciting,
    To stop gaps in his loose writing;
With such a deal of monstrous and forced action,
    As might make Bedlam a faction.
Nor made he his play for jests stol'n from each table,
    But makes jests to fit his fable;
And so presents quick comedy, refined
30   As best critics have designed.
The laws of time, place, persons he observeth;

3 **palates** taste   7 **still** always   9-12 **some . . . them** Jonson's theatrical enemies complained of the sharpness of his satire and taunted him with his slowness of composition   13 **this . . . creature** *i.e.,* the present play, *Volpone*   21 **custards** huge custards placed on the Lord Mayor's table at city feasts for the fool to jump into   22 **rout** mob   23 **gull** simpleton   **old ends** bits of proverbial wisdom, sententious couplets, etc.   26 **As . . . faction** As might turn the inmates of the London insane asylum into an enthusiastic audience   27 **stol'n . . . table** *i.e.,* plagiarized, and also dragged in without respect to the dramatic situation   29 **quick** live   31 **laws . . . persons** the so-called unities of time and place and the principle of decorum governing dramatic characters

From no needful rule he swerveth.
All gall and copperas from his ink he draineth;
Only a little salt remaineth,
Wherewith he'll rub your cheeks till, red with laughter,
They shall look fresh a week after.

VOLPONE, OR THE FOX

❦

Act One

[Volpone's house]

[Enter VOLPONE *and* MOSCA.]

VOLPONE. Good morning to the day; and next, my
    gold!—
Open the shrine, that I may see my saint.—[MOSCA *draws*
    a curtain and discovers a hoard of gold.]
Hail the world's soul, and mine! More glad than is
The teeming earth to see the longed-for sun
Peep through the horns of the celestial ram,
Am I, to view thy splendor darkening his;
That lying here, amongst my other hoards,
Show'st like a flame by night, or like the day
Struck out of chaos, when all darkness fled
Unto the center. O thou son of Sol,   10
But brighter than thy father, let me kiss,
With adoration, thee, and every relic
Of sacred treasure in this blessèd room.
Well did wise poets, by thy glorious name,
Title that age which they would have the best;
Thou being the best of things; and far transcending
All style of joy, in children, parents, friends,
Or any other waking dream on earth.
Thy looks when they to Venus did ascribe,
They should have giv'n her twenty thousand Cupids; 20
Such are thy beauties and our loves! Dear saint,
Riches, the dumb god, that giv'st all men tongues!
That canst do nought, and yet mak'st men do all things.
The price of souls! Even hell, with thee to boot,
Is made worth heaven! Thou art virtue, fame,

s.d. **Mosca** fly   5 **celestial ram** the zodiacal sign of Aries   10
Sol the sun   15 **that age** the golden age   19 **Thy . . . ascribe**
When they described Venus as "golden"

5

Honor, and all things else. Who can get thee,
He shall be noble, valiant, honest, wise——
   MOSCA. And what he will, sir. Riches are in fortune
A greater good than wisdom is in nature.
30   VOLPONE. True, my belovèd Mosca. Yet I glory
More in the cunning purchase of my wealth
Than in the glad possession, since I gain
No common way. I use no trade, no venture;
I wound no earth with plowshares, fat no beasts
To feed the shambles; have no mills for iron,
Oil, corn, or men, to grind 'em into powder;
I blow no subtle glass, expose no ships
To threat'nings of the furrow-facèd sea;
I turn no moneys in the public bank,
Nor usure private——
40   MOSCA.   No sir, nor devour
Soft prodigals. You shall ha' some will swallow
A melting heir as glibly as your Dutch
Will pills of butter, and ne'er purge for 't;
Tear forth the fathers of poor families
Out of their beds, and coffin them alive
In some kind, clasping prison, where their bones
May be forthcoming when the flesh is rotten.
But your sweet nature doth abhor these courses;
You loathe the widow's or the orphan's tears
50 Should wash your pavements, or their piteous cries
Ring in your roofs, and beat the air for vengeance.
   VOLPONE. Right, Mosca, I do loathe it.
   MOSCA.   And, besides, sir,
You are not like the thresher that doth stand
With a huge flail, watching a heap of corn,
And, hungry, dares not taste the smallest grain,
But feeds on mallows and such bitter herbs;
Nor like the merchant who hath filled his vaults
With Romagnía, and rich Candian wines,
Yet drinks the lees of Lombard's vinegar.
60 You will not lie in straw, whilst moths and worms
Feed on your sumptuous hangings and soft beds.
You know the use of riches, and dare give now
From that bright heap, to me, your poor observer,
Or to your dwarf, or your hermaphrodite,

---

31 **cunning purchase** ingenious methods of acquisition   33
venture commercial speculation   42 **Dutch** proverbially fond
of butter   58 **Romagnía** a sweet wine   **Candian** Cretan   63
observer follower

Your eunuch, or what other household trifle
Your pleasure allows maint'nance——
   VOLPONE.   Hold thee, Mosca,
Take of my hand; thou strik'st on truth in all,
And they are envious term thee parasite.
Call forth my dwarf, my eunuch, and my fool,
And let 'em make me sport! [*Exit* MOSCA.] What should I 70
   do
But cocker up my genius, and live free
To all delights my fortune calls me to?
I have no wife, no parent, child, ally,
To give my substance to; but whom I make
Must be my heir, and this makes men observe me.
This draws new clients daily to my house,
Women and men of every sex and age,
That bring me presents, send me plate, coin, jewels,
With hope that when I die—which they expect
Each greedy minute—it shall then return   80
Tenfold upon them; whilst some, covetous
Above the rest, seek to engross me whole,
And counter-work the one unto the other,
Contend in gifts, as they would seem, in love.
All which I suffer, playing with their hopes,
And am content to coin 'em into profit,
And look upon their kindness, and take more,
And look on that; still bearing them in hand,
Letting the cherry knock against their lips,
And draw it by their mouths, and back again.—   90
                      How now!

[*Re-enter* MOSCA *with* NANO, ANDROGYNO, *and* CASTRONE.]

   NANO. "Now, room for fresh gamesters, who do will you
     to know,
They do bring you neither play nor university show;
And therefore do entreat you that whatsoever they re-
     hearse
May not fare a whit the worse for the false pace of the
     verse.
If you wonder at this, you will wonder more ere we pass,
For know, here is enclosed the soul of Pythagoras,

65 **trifle** pet   71 **cocker** . . . **genius** indulge my disposition
75 **observe** pay court to   82 **engross** monopolize   88 **bearing**
. . . **hand** deluding them with false hopes   94 **false** . . . **verse**
the interlude is written in a loose four-stress line similar to
that in the old morality plays   96 **here** Nano points to
Androgyno

That juggler divine, as hereafter shall follow:
Which soul, fast and loose, sir, came first from Apollo,
And was breathed into Aethalides, Mercurius's son,
100 Where it had the gift to remember all that ever was done.
From thence it fled forth, and made quick transmigration
To goldy-locked Euphorbus, who was killed in good
        fashion
At the siege of old Troy, by the cuckold of Sparta.
Hermotimus was next—I find it in my charta—
To whom it did pass, where no sooner it was missing,
But with one Pyrrhus of Delos it learned to go a-fishing;
And thence did it enter the Sophist of Greece.
From Pythagore, she went into a beautiful piece,
Hight Aspasia the Meretrix; and the next toss of her
110 Was again of a whore she became a philosopher,
Crates the Cynic, as itself doth relate it.
Since, kings, knights, and beggars, knaves, lords, and fools
        gat it,
Besides ox and ass, camel, mule, goat, and brock,
In all which it hath spoke, as in the cobbler's cock.
But I come not here to discourse of that matter,
Or his one, two, or three, or his great oath, 'By Quater!'
His musics, his trigon, his golden thigh,
Or his telling how elements shift. But I
Would ask how of late thou hast suffered translation,
120 And shifted thy coat in these days of reformation?"
        ANDROGYNO. "Like one of the reformèd, a fool, as you
        see,
Counting all old doctrine heresy."
        NANO. "But not on thine own forbid meats hast thou
        ventured?"

99 **Aethalides** the first in a series of mythical and historical
persons who play host to the soul of Pythagoras in the follow-
ing lines. Their identities matter less than their diversity.
103 **cuckold of Sparta** Menelaus, husband of Helen   107
Sophist of Greece Pythagoras   109 **Hight** named   **Meretrix**
prostitute   113 **brock** badger   114 **cobbler's cock** In Lucian's
dialogue *The Cock*, on which this interlude is based, the soul
of Pythagoras, dwelling in a cock, relates his previous trans-
formations to his master, a cobbler   116 **Or . . . shift** The
numbers, the oath, the music, the trigon (triangle), golden
thigh, and shifting of elements all refer to Pythagorean doc-
trines and traditions   119 **how . . . reformation?** what shapes
have you assumed since the Reformation?   122 **old doctrine**
orthodox Roman Catholic doctrine, as opposed to the new
beliefs of the Reformation

ANDROGYNO. "On fish, when first a Carthusian I entered."
NANO. "Why, then thy dogmatical silence hath left
    thee?"
ANDROGYNO. "Of that an obstreperous lawyer bereft me."
NANO. "O wonderful change! When Sir Lawyer forsook
    thee,
For Pythagore's sake, what body then took thee?"
ANDROGYNO. "A good dull mule."
NANO.   "And how! By that means
Thou wert brought to allow of the eating of beans?"   130
ANDROGYNO. "Yes."
NANO. "But from the mule into whom didst thou pass?"
ANDROGYNO. "Into a very strange beast, by some writers
    called an ass;
By others a precise, pure, illuminate brother,
Of those devour flesh, and sometimes one another;
And will drop you forth a libel, or a sanctified lie,
Betwixt every spoonful of a nativity-pie."
NANO. "Now quit thee, 'fore heaven, of that profane na-
    tion,
And gently report thy next transmigration."
ANDROGYNO. "To the same that I am."
NANO.   "A creature of delight,
And, what is more than a fool, an hermaphrodite!   140
Now, pray thee, sweet soul, in all thy variation,
Which body wouldst thou choose to take up thy station?"
ANDROGYNO. "Troth, this I am in; even here would I
    tarry."
NANO. "'Cause here the delight of each sex thou canst
    vary?"
ANDROGYNO. "Alas, those pleasures be stale and forsaken.
No, 'tis your fool wherewith I am so taken,
The only one creature that I can call blessèd;
For all other forms I have proved most distressèd."
NANO. "Spoke true as thou wert in Pythagoras still.
This learnèd opinion we celebrate will,   150
Fellow eunuch, as behoves us, with all our wit and art,

124 **On fish . . . entered** The Carthusian order imposed strict
fasting rules, but not as strict as those of Pythagoras, who for-
bade even fish   125 **silence** Followers of Pythagoras observed
a five years' silence   130 **beans** Pythagoras prohibited the
eating of beans   133 **precise . . . brother** Puritan   **illuminate**
inspired   136 **nativity-pie** Christmas pie. Puritans objected
to the word "Christmas" because it contained the popish term
"mass."   138 **gently** civilly

To dignify that whereof ourselves are so great and special
    a part."

VOLPONE. Now, very, very pretty! Mosca, this
Was thy invention?
    MOSCA.   If it please my patron,
Not else.
    VOLPONE. It doth, good Mosca.
    MOSCA.   Then it was, sir.

SONG.

"Fools they are the only nation
    Worth men's envy or admiration,
    Free from care or sorrow taking,
    Selves and others merry making.
160   All they speak or do is sterling.
    Your fool he is your great man's darling,
    And your ladies' sport and pleasure;
    Tongue and bauble are his treasure.
    E'en his face begetteth laughter,
    And he speaks truth free from slaughter.
    He's the grace of every feast,
    And sometimes the chiefest guest;
    Hath his trencher and his stool,
    When wit waits upon the fool.
170   O, who would not be
        He, he, he?"

                            (One knocks without.)
    VOLPONE. Who's that? Away!—Look, Mosca.
                        [Exeunt NANO and CASTRONE.]
    MOSCA.   Fool, begone!
                            [Exit ANDROGYNO.]
'Tis Signor Voltore, the advocate;
I know him by his knock.
    VOLPONE.   Fetch me my gown,
My furs, and nightcaps; say my couch is changing;
And let him entertain himself a while
Without i' th' gallery. [Exit MOSCA.] Now, now my clients
Begin their visitation! Vulture, kite,
Raven, and gorcrow, all my birds of prey,
180 That think me turning carcass, now they come.
I am not for 'em yet. [Re-enter MOSCA.] How now! The
    news?
    MOSCA. A piece of plate, sir.

165 **free** . . . **slaughter** without penalty 168 **trencher** wooden
plate 179 **gorcrow** carrion crow

VOLPONE.   Of what bigness?

MOSCA.   Huge,
Massy, and antique, with your name inscribed
And arms engraven.

VOLPONE.   Good! And not a fox
Stretched on the earth, with fine delusive sleights,
Mocking a gaping crow? Ha, Mosca?

MOSCA.   Sharp, sir.

VOLPONE. Give me my furs. Why dost thou laugh so,
   man?

MOSCA. I cannot choose, sir, when I apprehend
What thoughts he has, without, now as he walks:
That this might be the last gift he should give;   190
That this would fetch you; if you died today,
And gave him all, what he should be tomorrow;
What large return would come of all his ventures;
How he should worshiped be, and reverenced;
Ride with his furs and foot-cloths, waited on
By herds of fools and clients; have clear way
Made for his mule, as lettered as himself;
Be called the great and learnèd advocate;
And then concludes there's nought impossible.

VOLPONE. Yes, to be learnèd, Mosca.

MOSCA.   O no, rich   200
Implies it. Hood an ass with reverend purple,
So you can hide his two ambitious ears,
And he shall pass for a cathedral doctor.

VOLPONE. My caps, my caps, good Mosca. Fetch him in.

MOSCA. Stay, sir, your ointment for your eyes.

VOLPONE.   That's true;
Dispatch, dispatch. I long to have possession
Of my new present.

MOSCA.   That and thousands more
I hope to see you lord of.

VOLPONE.   Thanks, kind Mosca.

MOSCA. And that, when I am lost in blended dust,
And hundred such as I am, in succession——   210

VOLPONE. Nay, that were too much, Mosca.

MOSCA.   You shall live
Still to delude these harpies.

VOLPONE.   Loving Mosca!
'Tis well; my pillow now, and let him enter.

                          [*Exit* MOSCA.]
Now, my feigned cough, my phthisic, and my gout,

197 **mule** legal officials rode on mules at this time in England
202 **ambitious** prominent   203 **cathedral doctor** physician who
holds a professorial chair

My apoplexy, palsy, and catarrhs,
Help, with your forcèd functions, this my posture,
Wherein this three year I have milked their hopes.
He comes; I hear him—Uh! [*Coughing.*] uh! uh! uh! O!

[*Re-enter* MOSCA *with* VOLTORE.]

MOSCA. You still are what you were, sir. Only you,
220 Of all the rest, are he, commands his love;
And you do wisely to preserve it thus
With early visitation, and kind notes
Of your good meaning to him, which, I know,
Cannot but come most grateful.—Patron! Sir!
Here's Signor Voltore is come——
    VOLPONE. [*Faintly.*]   What say you?
    MOSCA. Sir, Signor Voltore is come this morning
To visit you.
    VOLPONE. I thank him.
    MOSCA.   And hath brought
A piece of antique plate, bought of St. Mark,
With which he here presents you.
    VOLPONE.   He is welcome.
Pray him to come more often.
    MOSCA.   Yes.
230   VOLTORE.   What says he?
    MOSCA. He thanks you, and desires you see him often.
    VOLPONE. Mosca.
    MOSCA.   My patron!
    VOLPONE.   Bring him near; where is he?
I long to feel his hand.
    MOSCA.   The plate is here, sir.
    VOLTORE. How fare you, sir?
    VOLPONE.   I thank you, Signor Voltore.
Where is the plate? Mine eyes are bad.
    VOLTORE.   I'm sorry
To see you still thus weak.
    MOSCA. [*Aside.*]   —That he is not weaker.
    VOLPONE. You are too munificent.
    VOLTORE.   No, sir, would to heaven
I could as well give health to you, as that plate!
    VOLPONE. You give, sir, what you can. I thank you. Your
    love
240 Hath taste in this, and shall not be unanswered.

222 **notes** tokens   228 **of** . . . **Mark** at a goldsmith's shop in
the Piazza of St. Mark   240 **taste** savor

I pray you see me often.
VOLTORE.   Yes, I shall, sir.
VOLPONE. Be not far from me.
MOSCA.   Do you observe that, sir?
VOLPONE. Hearken unto me still. It will concern you.
MOSCA. You are a happy man, sir; know your good.
VOLPONE. I cannot now last long——
MOSCA.   —You are his heir, sir.
VOLTORE. Am I?
VOLPONE. I feel me going—Uh! uh! uh! uh!
I am sailing to my port—Uh! uh! uh! uh!
And I am glad I am so near my haven.
    MOSCA. Alas, kind gentleman! Well, we must all go——
VOLTORE. But, Mosca——
MOSCA.   Age will conquer.
VOLTORE.   Pray thee, hear me. 250
Am I inscribed his heir for certain?
MOSCA.   Are you!
I do beseech you, sir, you will vouchsafe
To write me i' your family. All my hopes
Depend upon your worship. I am lost,
Except the rising sun do shine on me.
    VOLTORE. It shall both shine and warm thee, Mosca.
MOSCA.   Sir,
I am a man that have not done your love
All the worst offices: here I wear your keys,
See all your coffers and your caskets locked,
Keep the poor inventory of your jewels,   260
Your plate, and moneys; am your steward, sir,
Husband your goods here.
    VOLTORE.   But am I sole heir?
    MOSCA. Without a partner, sir, confirmed this morning;
The wax is warm yet, and the ink scarce dry
Upon the parchment.
    VOLTORE.   Happy, happy me!
By what good chance, sweet Mosca?
    MOSCA.   Your desert, sir;
I know no second cause.
    VOLTORE.   Thy modesty
Is loath to know it; well, we shall requite it.
    MOSCA. He ever liked your course, sir; that first took him.
I oft have heard him say how he admired   270
Men of your large profession, that could speak

243 **still** further   253 **write . . . family** make me a servant in
your household   271 **large** liberal

To every cause, and things mere contraries,
Till they were hoarse again, yet all be law;
That, with most quick agility, could turn
And re-turn, make knots and undo them,
Give forkèd counsel, take provoking gold
On either hand, and put it up. These men,
He knew, would thrive with their humility.
And, for his part, he thought he should be blest
280 To have his heir of such a suffering spirit,
So wise, so grave, of so perplexed a tongue,
And loud withal, that would not wag, nor scarce
Lie still, without a fee; when every word
Your worship but lets fall, is a chequìn!

(Another knocks.)

—Who's that? One knocks; I would not have you seen, sir.
And yet—pretend you came and went in haste;
I'll fashion an excuse. And, gentle sir,
When you do come to swim in golden lard,
Up to the arms in honey, that your chin
290 Is borne up stiff with fatness of the flood,
Think on your vassal; but remember me.
I ha' not been your worst of clients.
    VOLTORE.   Mosca—
    MOSCA. When will you have your inventory brought, sir?
Or see a copy of the will?—Anon!—
I'll bring 'em to you, sir. Away, begone,
Put business i' your face.   [*Exit* VOLTORE.]
    VOLPONE. [*Springing up.*] Excellent, Mosca!
Come hither, let me kiss thee.
    MOSCA.   Keep you still, sir.
Here is Corbaccio.
    VOLPONE.   Set the plate away.
The vulture's gone, and the old raven's come.
300   MOSCA. Betake you to your silence, and your sleep.—
Stand there and multiply. [*Adding the plate to the hoard.*]
        —Now shall we see
A wretch who is indeed more impotent
Than this can feign to be, yet hopes to hop
Over his grave.

[*Enter* CORBACCIO.]

272 **mere** absolute 276 **provoking** both "exciting" to the
lawyer, and designed as a bribe 281 **perplexed** entangled in
contradictions 284 **chequìn** Venetian gold coin 294 **Anon!**
Right away! shouted to Corbaccio, who has knocked for
entrance 299 **vulture** Voltore **raven** Corbaccio

Signor Corbaccio!

You're very welcome, sir.

CORBACCIO. How does your patron?

MOSCA. Troth, as he did, sir; no amends.

CORBACCIO. What! Mends he?

MOSCA. No, sir, he is rather worse.

CORBACCIO. That's well. Where is he?

MOSCA. Upon his couch, sir, newly fall'n asleep.

CORBACCIO. Does he sleep well?

MOSCA. No wink, sir, all this night
Nor yesterday, but slumbers.

CORBACCIO. Good! He should take 31(
Some counsel of physicians: I have brought him
An opiate here, from mine own doctor.

MOSCA. He will not hear of drugs.

CORBACCIO. Why? I myself
Stood by while't was made, saw all th' ingredients;
And know it cannot but most gently work.
My life for his, 'tis but to make him sleep.

VOLPONE. [*Aside.*]—Ay, his last sleep, if he would take
it.

MOSCA. Sir,
He has no faith in physic.

CORBACCIO. Say you? Say you?

MOSCA. He has no faith in physic; he does think
Most of your doctors are the greater danger, 320
And worse disease, t' escape. I often have
Heard him protest that your physician
Should never be his heir.

CORBACCIO. Not I his heir?

MOSCA. Not your physician, sir.

CORBACCIO. O no, no, no.
I do not mean it.

MOSCA. No, sir, nor their fees
He cannot brook; he says they flay a man
Before they kill him.

CORBACCIO. Right, I do conceive you.

MOSCA. And then, they do it by experiment;
For which the law not only doth absolve 'em,
But gives them great reward; and he is loath 330
To hire his death so.

CORBACCIO. It is true, they kill
With as much licence as a judge.

310 **slumbers** dozes 318 **physic** medicine 327 **conceive** understand 328 **by experiment** as an experiment

MOSCA. Nay, more;
For he but kills, sir, where the law condemns,
And these can kill him too.
CORBACCIO. Ay, or me,
Or any man. How does his apoplex?
Is that strong on him still?
MOSCA. Most violent.
His speech is broken and his eyes are set,
His face drawn longer than 'twas wont——
CORBACCIO. How? How?
Stronger than he was wont?
MOSCA. No, sir; his face
Drawn longer than 'twas wont.
CORBACCIO. O, good!
840 MOSCA. His mouth
Is ever gaping, and his eyelids hang.
CORBACCIO. Good.
MOSCA. A freezing numbness stiffens all his joints,
And makes the color of his flesh like lead.
CORBACCIO. 'Tis good.
MOSCA. His pulse beats slow and dull.
CORBACCIO. Good symptoms still.
MOSCA. And from his brain——
CORBACCIO. Ha! How? Not from his brain?
MOSCA. Yes, sir, and from his brain——
CORBACCIO. I conceive you; good.
MOSCA. Flows a cold sweat, with a continual rheum,
Forth the resolvèd corners of his eyes.
CORBACCIO. Is't possible? Yet I am better, ha!
850 How does he with the swimming of his head?
MOSCA. O, sir, 'tis past the scotomy; he now
Hath lost his feeling, and hath left to snort.
You hardly can perceive him, that he breathes.
CORBACCIO. Excellent, excellent! Sure I shall outlast him!
This makes me young again a score of years.
MOSCA. I was a-coming for you, sir.
CORBACCIO. Has he made his will?
What has he giv'n me?
MOSCA. No, sir.
CORBACCIO. Nothing! Ha?
MOSCA. He has not made his will, sir.
CORBACCIO. Oh, oh, oh.
What then did Voltore, the lawyer, here?

347 **rheum** watery discharge 348 **Forth** Forth from **resolvèd**
dissolved 351 **scotomy** dizziness 352 **left** ceased

Mosca. He smelt a carcass, sir, when he but heard   360
My master was about his testament;
As I did urge him to it, for your good——
      Corbaccio. He came unto him, did he? I thought so.
Mosca. Yes, and presented him this piece of plate.
Corbaccio. To be his heir?
      Mosca.   I do not know, sir.
      Corbaccio.   True,
I know it too.
      Mosca. [Aside.] By your own scale, sir.
      Corbaccio.   Well,
I shall prevent him yet. See, Mosca, look,
Here I have brought a bag of bright chequìns,
Will quite weigh down his plate.
      Mosca.   Yea, marry, sir,   370
This is true physic, this your sacred medicine!
No talk of opiates to this great elixir!
      Corbaccio. 'Tis *aurum palpabile*, if not *potabile*.
Mosca. It shall be ministered to him in his bowl.
      Corbaccio. Ay, do, do, do.
      Mosca.   Most blessèd cordial!
This will recover him.
      Corbaccio.   Yes, do, do, do.
Mosca. I think it were not best, sir.
      Corbaccio.   What?
      Mosca.   To recover him.
      Corbaccio. O no, no, no, by no means.
      Mosca.   Why, sir, this
Will work some strange effect, if he but feel it.
      Corbaccio. 'Tis true, therefore forbear; I'll take my ven-
      ture.
Give me 't again.
      Mosca.   At no hand, pardon me;   380
You shall not do yourself that wrong, sir. I
Will so advise you, you shall have it all.
      Corbaccio. How?
      Mosca. All, sir, 'tis your right, your own; no man
Can claim a part. 'Tis yours without a rival,
Decreed by destiny.
      Corbaccio.   How, how, good Mosca?

367 **prevent him** be ahead of him   369 **marry** indeed   372
'**Tis . . . potabile** It is gold that can be felt, if not drunk.
Aurum potabile, a dissolved gold compound, was thought to
be a highly effective remedy.   379 **venture** investment, *i.e.,*
the bag of gold pieces

Mosca. I'll tell you, sir. This fit he shall recover—
Corbaccio. I do conceive you.
Mosca.   And on first advantage
Of his gained sense, will I re-importune him
Unto the making of his testament;
And show him this. [*Pointing to the bag of coins.*]
    Corbaccio.   Good, good.
390   Mosca.   'Tis better yet,
If you will hear, sir.
    Corbaccio.   Yes, with all my heart.
    Mosca. Now would I counsel you, make home with
      speed;
There, frame a will, whereto you shall inscribe
My master your sole heir.
    Corbaccio.   And disinherit
My son?
    Mosca. O, sir, the better; for that color
Shall make it much more taking.
    Corbaccio.   O, but color?
    Mosca. This will, sir, you shall send it unto me.
Now, when I come to enforce, as I will do,
Your cares, your watchings, and your many prayers,
400 Your more than many gifts, your this day's present;
And last, produce your will, where, without thought
Or least regard unto your proper issue,
A son so brave and highly meriting,
The stream of your diverted love hath thrown you
Upon my master, and made him your heir;
He cannot be so stupid, or stone-dead,
But out of conscience and mere gratitude——
    Corbaccio. He must pronounce me his?
    Mosca.   'Tis true.
    Corbaccio.   This plot
Did I think on before.
    Mosca.   I do believe it.
    Corbaccio. Do you not believe it?
    Mosca.   Yes, sir.
410   Corbaccio.   Mine own project.
    Mosca. Which, when he hath done, sir——
    Corbaccio.   Published me his heir?
    Mosca. And you so certain to survive him——

388 **gained sense** regained consciousness   395 **color** appearance   396 **taking** attractive   398 **enforce** urge   399 **watchings** bedside vigils   402 **proper** own   403 **brave** fine   404 **diverted** *i.e.*, from your own son

CORBACCIO.   Ay.
MOSCA. Being so lusty a man——
CORBACCIO.   'Tis true.
MOSCA.   Yes, sir——
CORBACCIO. I thought on that, too. See, how he should
  be
The very organ to express my thoughts!
  MOSCA. You have not only done yourself a good——
  CORBACCIO. But multiplied it on my son!
  MOSCA.   'Tis right, sir.
  CORBACCIO. Still my invention.
  MOSCA.   'Las, sir! Heaven knows,
It hath been all my study, all my care,—
I e'en grow gray withal—how to work things——   420
  CORBACCIO. I do conceive, sweet Mosca.
  MOSCA.   You are he
For whom I labor here.
  CORBACCIO.   Ay, do, do, do!
I'll straight about it.
  MOSCA. [*Aside.*] Rook go with you, raven!
  CORBACCIO. I know thee honest.
  MOSCA. [*Aside.*]   You do lie, sir!
  CORBACCIO.   And——
  MOSCA. [*Aside.*] Your knowledge is no better than your
    ears, sir.
  CORBACCIO. I do not doubt to be a father to thee.
  MOSCA. [*Aside.*] Nor I to gull my brother of his blessing.
  CORBACCIO. I may ha' my youth restored to me, why
    not?
  MOSCA. [*Aside.*] Your worship is a precious ass!
  CORBACCIO.   What say'st thou?
  MOSCA. I do desire your worship to make haste, sir.   430
  CORBACCIO. 'Tis done, 'tis done; I go.   [*Exit.*]
  VOLPONE. [*Leaping from his couch.*] O, I shall burst!
Let out my sides, let out my sides——
  MOSCA.   Contain
Your flux of laughter, sir. You know this hope
Is such a bait, it covers any hook.
  VOLPONE. O, but thy working and thy placing it!
I cannot hold; good rascal, let me kiss thee!
I never knew thee in so rare a humor.
  MOSCA. Alas, sir, I but do as I am taught;

423 **Rook . . . you** Be rooked, *i.e.,* duped   427 **gull** cheat
433 **flux** great outburst   437 **humor** mood

Follow your grave instructions; give 'em words;
440 Pour oil into their ears, and send them hence.
    VOLPONE. 'Tis true, 'tis true. What a rare punishment
Is avarice to itself!
    MOSCA.   Ay, with our help, sir.
    VOLPONE. So many cares, so many maladies,
So many fears attending on old age,
Yea, death so often called on, as no wish
Can be more frequent with 'em, their limbs faint,
Their senses dull, their seeing, hearing, going,
All dead before them; yea, their very teeth,
Their instruments of eating, failing them;
450 Yet this is reckoned life! Nay, here was one,
Is now gone home, that wishes to live longer!
Feels not his gout, nor palsy; feigns himself
Younger by scores of years, flatters his age
With confident belying it, hopes he may
With charms, like Aeson, have his youth restored;
And with these thoughts so battens, as if fate
Would be as easily cheated on as he,
And all turns air! (*Another knocks.*) Who's that there,
    now? A third?
    MOSCA. Close, to your couch again. I hear his voice.
It is Corvino, our spruce merchant.
460   VOLPONE. [*Lies down as before.*] Dead.
    MOSCA. Another bout, sir, with your eyes.—Who's there?

[*Enter* CORVINO.]

Signor Corvino! Come most wished for! O,
How happy were you, if you knew it, now!
    CORVINO. Why? What? Wherein?
    MOSCA.   The tardy hour is come, sir.
    CORVINO. He is not dead?
    MOSCA.   Not dead, sir, but as good;
He knows no man.
    CORVINO.   How shall I do, then?
    MOSCA.   Why, sir?
    CORVINO. I have brought him here a pearl.
    MOSCA.   Perhaps he has
So much remembrance left as to know you, sir;

439 **give . . . words** deceive them with plausible speeches
447 **going** walking   455 **Aeson** father of Jason, restored to
youth by the magic of his son's wife, Medea   460 **Corvino**
crow   461 **Another . . . eyes** Another application of eye ointment to renew the disguise

He still calls on you; nothing but your name
Is in his mouth. Is your pearl orient, sir?   470
   CORVINO. Venice was never owner of the like.
   VOLPONE. [*Faintly.*] Signor Corvino!
   MOSCA.   Hark.
   VOLPONE.   Signor Corvino!
   MOSCA. He calls you; step and give it him.—He's here,
     sir,
And he has brought you a rich pearl.
   CORVINO.   How do you, sir?—
Tell him it doubles the twelfth carat.
   MOSCA.   Sir,
He cannot understand; his hearing's gone;
And yet it comforts him to see you——
   CORVINO.   Say
I have a diamond for him, too.
   MOSCA.   Best show't, sir,
Put it into his hand; 'tis only there
He apprehends. He has his feeling yet.   480
See how he grasps it!
   CORVINO.   'Las, good gentleman!
How pitiful the sight is!
   MOSCA.   Tut, forget, sir.
The weeping of an heir should still be laughter
Under a visor.
   CORVINO.   Why, am I his heir?
   MOSCA. Sir, I am sworn, I may not show the will
Till he be dead; but here has been Corbaccio,
Here has been Voltore, here were others too,
I cannot number 'em, they were so many,
All gaping here for legacies; but I,
Taking the vantage of his naming you,   490
"Signor Corvino," "Signor Corvino," took
Paper and pen and ink, and there I asked him
Whom he would have his heir? "Corvino!" Who
Should be executor? "Corvino!" And
To any question he was silent to,
I still interpreted the nods he made,
Through weakness, for consent; and sent home th' others,
Nothing bequeathed them but to cry and curse.
   CORVINO. O my dear Mosca! (*They embrace.*) Does he
     not perceive us?
   MOSCA. No more than a blind harper. He knows no man, 500

---

469 **still** constantly   470 **orient** of purest luster   484 **visor**
countenance of feigned grief

No face of friend nor name of any servant,
Who 'twas that fed him last or gave him drink;
Not those he hath begotten or brought up
Can he remember.
    CORVINO.   Has he children?
    MOSCA.   Bastards,
Some dozen or more that he begot on beggars,
Gypsies, and Jews, and black-moors, when he was drunk.
Knew you not that, sir? 'Tis the common fable.
The dwarf, the fool, the eunuch, are all his;
He's the true father of his family,
510 In all save me—but he has giv'n 'em nothing.
    CORVINO. That's well, that's well! Art sure he does not
        hear us?
    MOSCA. Sure, sir? Why, look you, credit your own sense.—
        [*Shouts in* VOLPONE'S *ear.*]
The pox approach, and add to your diseases,
If it would send you hence the sooner, sir!
For your incontinence it hath deserved it
Throughly and throughly, and the plague to boot!—
You may come near, sir.—Would you would once close
Those filthy eyes of yours, that flow with slime,
Like two frog-pits; and those same hanging cheeks,
520 Covered with hide instead of skin—nay, help, sir.——
That look like frozen dish-clouts set on end!
    CORVINO. Or like an old smoked wall, on which the rain
Ran down in streaks!
    MOSCA.   Excellent, sir! Speak out;
You may be louder yet. A culverin
Dischargèd in his ear would hardly bore it.
    CORVINO. His nose is like a common sewer, still running.
    MOSCA. 'Tis good! And what his mouth?
    CORVINO.   A very draught.
    MOSCA. O, stop it up——
    CORVINO.   By no means.
    MOSCA.   Pray you let me.
Faith, I could stifle him rarely with a pillow,
530 As well as any woman that should keep him.
    CORVINO. Do as you will, but I'll be gone.
    MOSCA.   Be so;
It is your presence makes him last so long.
    CORVINO. I pray you use no violence.
    MOSCA.   No, sir? Why?

513 **pox** syphilis   520 **help** *i.e.,* to insult him   524 **culverin**
cannon   530 **keep** watch over

Why should you be thus scrupulous, pray you, sir?
  CORVINO. Nay, at your discretion.
  MOSCA.   Well, good sir, begone.
  CORVINO. I will not trouble him now to take my pearl.
  MOSCA. Pooh! Nor your diamond. What a needless care
Is this afflicts you? Is not all here yours?
Am not I here, whom you have made your creature,
That owe my being to you?
  CORVINO.   Grateful Mosca!   540
Thou art my friend, my fellow, my companion,
My partner, and shalt share in all my fortunes.
  MOSCA. Excepting one.
  CORVINO.   What's that?
  MOSCA.   Your gallant wife, sir.
                        [*Exit* CORVINO.]
Now is he gone. We had no other means
To shoot him hence, but this.
  VOLPONE.   My divine Mosca!
Thou hast today out-gone thyself. (*Another knocks.*)
    Who's there?
I will be troubled with no more. Prepare
Me music, dances, banquets, all delights;
The Turk is not more sensual in his pleasures
Than will Volpone. Let me see, a pearl!   550
A diamond! Plate! Chequins! Good morning's purchase.
Why, this is better than rob churches yet!
Or fat, by eating once a month a man——
Who is't?
  MOSCA. The beauteous Lady Wouldbe, sir,
Wife to the English knight, Sir Politic Wouldbe,—
This is the style, sir, is directed me—
Hath sent to know how you have slept tonight,
And if you would be visited?
  VOLPONE.   Not now.
Some three hours hence——
  MOSCA.   I told the squire so much.
  VOLPONE. When I am high with mirth and wine, then, 560
    then!
'Fore heaven, I wonder at the desperate valor
Of the bold English, that they dare let loose
Their wives to all encounters!
  MOSCA.   Sir, this knight
Had not his name for nothing; he is politic,
And knows, howe'er his wife affect strange airs,

551 **purchase** loot   553 **fat** grow fat   564 **politic crafty**

She hath not yet the face to be dishonest.
But had she Signor Corvino's wife's face——
    VOLPONE. Has she so rare a face?
    MOSCA.   O, sir, the wonder,
The blazing star of Italy! A wench
570 O' the first year! A beauty ripe as harvest!
Whose skin is whiter than a swan all over!
Than silver, snow, or lilies! A soft lip,
Would tempt you to eternity of kissing!
And flesh that melteth in the touch to blood!
Bright as your gold, and lovely as your gold!
    VOLPONE. Why had not I known this before?
    MOSCA.   Alas, sir,
Myself but yesterday discovered it.
    VOLPONE. How might I see her?
    MOSCA.   O, not possible.
She's kept as warily as is your gold;
580 Never does come abroad, never takes air
But at a window. All her looks are sweet
As the first grapes or cherries, and are watched
As near as they are.
    VOLPONE.   I must see her!
    MOSCA.   Sir,
There is a guard of ten spies thick upon her—
All his whole household—each of which is set
Upon his fellow, and have all their charge,
When he goes out, when he comes in, examined.
    VOLPONE. I will go see her, though but at her window.
    MOSCA. In some disguise, then.
    VOLPONE.   That is true. I must
590 Maintain mine own shape still the same. We'll think.
                                      [*Exeunt.*]

Act Two

SCENE ONE

[*Before Corvino's house, off the Piazza of St. Mark*]

[*Enter* SIR POLITIC WOULDBE *and* PEREGRINE.]

    SIR POLITIC. Sir, to a wise man, all the world's his soil.

566 **face** "audacity," in addition to the usual meaning **dishonest** unfaithful   583 **near** closely   586 **charge** fixed instructions   1 **soil** native place

It is not Italy, nor France, nor Europe,
That must bound me, if my fates call me forth.
Yet I protest, it is no salt desire
Of seeing countries, shifting a religion,
Nor any disaffection to the state
Where I was bred, and unto which I owe
My dearest plots, hath brought me out; much less
That idle, antique, stale, grey-headed project
Of knowing men's minds and manners, with Ulysses;   1(
But a peculiar humor of my wife's,
Laid for this height of Venice, to observe,
To quote, to learn the language, and so forth——
I hope you travel, sir, with license?

PEREGRINE.   Yes.

SIR POLITIC. I dare the safelier converse——How long, sir,
Since you left England?

PEREGRINE.   Seven weeks.

SIR POLITIC.   So lately!
You ha' not been with my Lord Ambassador?

PEREGRINE. Not yet, sir.

SIR POLITIC.   Pray you, what news, sir, vents
our climate?
I heard last night a most strange thing reported
By some of my Lord's followers, and I long   20
To hear how 'twill be seconded!

PEREGRINE.   What was 't, sir?

SIR POLITIC. Marry, sir, of a raven that should build
In a ship royal of the King's.

PEREGRINE. [*Aside*.]   —This fellow,
Does he gull me, trow, or is gulled?—Your name, sir?

SIR POLITIC. My name is Politic Wouldbe.

PEREGRINE. [*Aside*.]   —O, that speaks him.—
A knight, sir?

SIR POLITIC. A poor knight, sir.

PEREGRINE.   Your lady
Lies here in Venice, for intelligence
Of tires and fashions and behavior
Among the courtesans? The fine Lady Wouldbe?

4 **salt** excessive   10 **Ulysses** celebrated as a traveler   11 **humor**
whim   12 **Laid . . . height** directed toward this latitude   13
quote note down   14 **license** official permission   18 **vents** cir-
culates   21 **seconded** confirmed   22 **should build** was reported
to have built (its nest)   24 **gull me** make a fool of me   27
intelligence information   28 **tires** dress

30　Sɪʀ Poʟɪᴛɪᴄ. Yes, sir, the spider and the bee oft-times
Suck from one flower.
　　Peʀᴇɢʀɪɴᴇ.　　　　Good Sir Politic,
I cry you mercy! I have heard much of you.
'Tis true, sir, of your raven.
　　Sɪʀ Poʟɪᴛɪᴄ.　　　　　On your knowledge?
　　Peʀᴇɢʀɪɴᴇ. Yes, and your lion's whelping in the Tower.
　　Sɪʀ Poʟɪᴛɪᴄ. Another whelp?
　　Peʀᴇɢʀɪɴᴇ.　　　　　　Another, sir.
　　Sɪʀ Poʟɪᴛɪᴄ.　　　　　　　　Now, heaven!
What prodigies be these? The fires at Berwick!
And the new star! These things concurring, strange
And full of omen! Saw you those meteors?
　　Peʀᴇɢʀɪɴᴇ. I did, sir.
　　Sɪʀ Poʟɪᴛɪᴄ.　　　　Fearful! Pray you, sir, confirm me,
40　Were there three porpoises seen above the bridge,
As they give out?
　　Peʀᴇɢʀɪɴᴇ.　　Six, and a sturgeon, sir.
　　Sɪʀ Poʟɪᴛɪᴄ. I am astonished!
　　Peʀᴇɢʀɪɴᴇ.　　　　　　Nay, sir, be not so;
I'll tell you a greater prodigy than these——
　　Sɪʀ Poʟɪᴛɪᴄ. What should these things portend?
　　Peʀᴇɢʀɪɴᴇ.　　　　　　　　The very day—
Let me be sure—that I put forth from London,
There was a whale discovered in the river,
As high as Woolwich, that had waited there,
Few know how many months, for the subversion
Of the Stode fleet.
　　Sɪʀ Poʟɪᴛɪᴄ.　　Is't possible? Believe it,
50　'Twas either sent from Spain, or the Archduke's!
Spinola's whale, upon my life, my credit!
Will they not leave these projects? Worthy sir,
Some other news.
　　Peʀᴇɢʀɪɴᴇ.　　Faith, Stone the fool is dead,
And they do lack a tavern-fool extremely.
　　Sɪʀ Poʟɪᴛɪᴄ. Is Mas' Stone dead?
　　Peʀᴇɢʀɪɴᴇ.　　　　　　He's dead, sir; why, I hope
You thought him not immortal? [Aside.]—O, this knight,

32 I . . . mercy I beg your pardon　34 Tower the Tower of
London　36 fires at Berwick reports of ghost armies firing on
the Scottish border　49 Stode city near Hamburg, Germany
50 Archduke Governor of the Spanish Netherlands　51 Spinola's whale Spinola, Spanish general, popularly credited with
having devised various bizarre secret weapons, such as a whale
hired to drown London by discharging Thames water on it
55 Mas' Master

Were he well known, would be a precious thing
To fit our English stage. He that should write
But such a fellow, should be thought to feign
Extremely, if not maliciously.

SIR POLITIC.   Stone dead!   60

PEREGRINE. Dead. Lord, how deeply, sir, you apprehend
    it!
He was no kinsman to you?

SIR POLITIC.   That I know of.
Well, that same fellow was an unknown fool.

PEREGRINE. And yet you knew him, it seems?

SIR POLITIC.   I did so. **Sir,**
I knew him one of the most dangerous heads
Living within the state, and so I held him.

PEREGRINE. Indeed, sir?

SIR POLITIC.   While he lived, in action.
He has received weekly intelligence,
Upon my knowledge, out of the Low Countries,
For all parts of the world, in cabbages;   70
And those dispensed again t'ambassadors,
In oranges, muskmelons, apricots,
Lemons, pomecitrons, and suchlike; sometimes
In Colchester oysters, and your Selsey cockles.

PEREGRINE. You make me wonder!

SIR POLITIC.   Sir, upon my knowledge.
Nay, I have observed him, at your public ordinary,
Take his advertisement from a traveler—
A concealed statesman—in a trencher of meat;
And instantly, before the meal was done,
Convey an answer in a toothpick.

PEREGRINE.   Strange!   80
How could this be, sir?

SIR POLITIC.   Why, the meat was cut
So like his character, and so laid, as he
Must easily read the cipher.

PEREGRINE.   I have heard
He could not read, sir.

SIR POLITIC.   So 'twas given out,

61 **apprehend it** take it to heart   68-80 **He . . . toothpick** a burlesque of the fanciful methods attributed to spies for receiving and transmitting secret information   71 **dispensed** conveyed out   73 **pomecitrons** fruits similar to lemons   76 **ordinary** tavern   77 **advertisement** information   78 **concealed** disguised   81 **meat . . . cipher** the meat was cut into shapes to resemble the "character" or "cipher"—the secret code—of the spy to whom it was served

In policy, by those that did employ him.
But he could read, and had your languages,
And to 't, as sound a noddle——
    PEREGRINE.   I have heard, sir,
That your baboons were spies, and that they were
A kind of subtle nation near to China.
90   SIR POLITIC. Ay, ay, your *Mamaluchi*. Faith, they had
Their hand in a French plot or two; but they
Were so extremely given to women, as
They made discovery of all. Yet I
Had my advices here, on Wednesday last,
From one of their own coat, they were returned,
Made their relations, as the fashion is,
And now stand fair for fresh employment.
    PEREGRINE. [*Aside.*]   —Heart!
This Sir Poll will be ignorant of nothing.—
It seems, sir, you know all.
    SIR POLITIC.   Not all, sir, but
100 I have some general notions. I do love
To note and to observe. Though I live out,
Free from the active torrent, yet I'd mark
The currents and the passages of things
For mine own private use; and know the ebbs
And flows of state.
    PEREGRINE.   Believe it, sir, I hold
Myself in no small tie unto my fortunes,
For casting me thus luckily upon you;
Whose knowledge, if your bounty equal it,
May do me great assistance, in instruction
110 For my behavior and my bearing, which
Is yet so rude and raw——
    SIR POLITIC.   Why? Came you forth
Empty of rules for travel?
    PEREGRINE.   Faith, I had
Some common ones, from out that vulgar grammar,
Which he that cried Italian to me, taught me.
    SIR POLITIC. Why, this it is that spoils all our brave
      bloods:

85 **in policy** for reasons of state   86 **had . . . languages** knew
languages 87 **noddle** head 90 **Mamaluchi** properly a term
for converted slaves in Moslem countries 93 **made . . . of**
betrayed 94 **advices** dispatches 95 **coat** class 97 **made . . .
relations** submitted their reports 106 **in . . . tie** very much
indebted 113 **vulgar** common 115 **brave bloods** fine young
gentlemen

Trusting our hopeful gentry unto pedants,
Fellows of outside, and mere bark. You seem
To be a gentleman of ingenuous race——
I not profess it, but my fate hath been
To be where I have been consulted with,   120
In this high kind, touching some great men's sons,
Persons of blood and honor——

[*Enter* MOSCA *and* NANO *disguised, followed by* GREGE.]

PEREGRINE.   Who be these, sir?
MOSCA. Under that window, there 't must be. The same.
SIR POLITIC. Fellows to mount a bank! Did your instruc-
    tor
In the dear tongues never discourse to you
Of the Italian mountebanks?
PEREGRINE.   Yes, sir.
SIR POLITIC.   Why,
Here shall you see one.
PEREGRINE.   They are quacksalvers,
Fellows that live by venting oils and drugs.
SIR POLITIC. Was that the character he gave you of them?
PEREGRINE. As I remember.
SIR POLITIC.   Pity his ignorance.   130
They are the only knowing men of Europe!
Great general scholars, excellent physicians,
Most admired statesmen, professed favorites,
And cabinet counsellors to the greatest princes!
The only languaged men of all the world!
PEREGRINE. And I have heard they are most lewd impos-
    tors,
Made all of terms and shreds; no less beliers
Of great men's favors, than their own vile med'cines;
Which they will utter, upon monstrous oaths,
Selling that drug for twopence, ere they part,   140
Which they have valued at twelve crowns before.
SIR POLITIC. Sir, calumnies are answered best with si-
    lence.
Yourself shall judge.—Who is it mounts, my friends?
MOSCA. Scoto of Mantua, sir.

118 **ingenuous** noble   119 **I . . . it** I do not boast of it
121 **In . . . kind** In this important matter   125 **dear tongues**
esteemed languages   136 **lewd** ignorant and unprincipled   137
terms technical words   **shreds** quotations, proverbs, sententious
remarks, etc.   139 **utter** sell   144 **Scoto of Mantua** celebrated
Italian comedian

Sir Politic.   Is't he? Nay, then
I'll proudly promise, sir, you shall behold
Another man than has been fancied to you.
I wonder yet that he should mount his bank
Here in this nook, that has been wont t' appear
In face of the Piazza. Here he comes!

[*Enter* Volpone *disguised as a mountebank.*]

Volpone. Mount, zany.
150   Grege.   Follow, follow, follow, follow, follow!
Sir Politic. See how the people follow him! He's a man
May write ten thousand crowns in bank here. Note,
Mark but his gesture. I do use to observe
The state he keeps in getting up.
Peregrine.   'Tis worth it, sir.
Volpone. "Most noble gentlemen, and my worthy pa-
trons: It may seem strange that I, your Scoto Mantuano,
who was ever wont to fix my bank in face of the public
Piazza, near the shelter of the portico to the *Procuratía*,[1]
should now, after eight months' absence from this illustrious city of Venice, humbly retire myself into an obscure
nook of the Piazza."
Sir Politic. Did not I now object the same?
Peregrine.   Peace, sir.
Volpone. "Let me tell you: I am not—as your Lombard
proverb saith—cold on my feet,[2] or content to part with
my commodities at a cheaper rate than I accustomed; look
not for it. Nor that the calumnious reports of that impudent
detractor and shame to our profession—Alessandro Buttone,[3] I mean—who gave out in public, I was condemned
a *sforzato*[4] to the galleys, for poisoning the Cardinal Bembo's—[5] cook, hath at all attached,[6] much less dejected me.
No, no, worthy gentlemen, to tell you true, I cannot endure
to see the rabble of these ground *ciarlatani*,[7] that spread
their cloaks on the pavement as if they meant to do feats
of activity,[8] and then come in lamely, with their moldy

150 **zany** clown who mimics the antics of another clown   154
state he keeps ceremony he observes   [1] **Procuratía** residence of
the officials of St. Mark's   [2] **cold . . . feet** reduced to desperation by poverty   [3] **Buttone** a fellow mountebank   [4] **sforzato**
convict   [5] **Bembo's**— the dash represents an insinuation. Volpone pretends to hesitate in order to avoid saying "whore" or
"mistress."   [6] **attached** made me subject to legal action
[7] **ground ciarlatani** common mountebanks   [8] **feats of activity**
acrobatics

tales out of Boccaccio, like stale Tabarine,[9] the fabulist;[10] some of them discoursing their travels, and of their tedious captivity in the Turk's galleys, when indeed—were the truth known—they were the Christian's galleys, where very temperately they eat[11] bread and drunk water, as a wholesome penance, enjoined them by their confessors, for base pilferies."

SIR POLITIC. Note but his bearing, and contempt of these.

VOLPONE. "These turdy-facy-nasty-paty-lousy-fartical rogues, with one poor groatsworth of unprepared antimony, finely wrapped up in several [12] scartoccios,[13] are able very well to kill their twenty a week, and play. Yet these meager, starved spirits, who have half stopped the organs of their minds with earthly oppilations,[14] want not their favorers among your shrivelled, salad-eating artisans, who are overjoyed that they may have their half-pe'rth[15] of physic; though it purge 'em into another world, 't makes no matter."

SIR POLITIC. Excellent! Ha' you heard better language, sir?

VOLPONE. "Well, let 'em go. And, gentlemen, honorable gentlemen, know that for this time our bank, being thus removed from the clamors of the canaglia,[16] shall be the scene of pleasure and delight; for I have nothing to sell, little or nothing to sell."

SIR POLITIC. I told you, sir, his end.

PEREGRINE.   You did so, sir.

VOLPONE. "I protest, I and my six servants are not able to make of this precious liquor so fast as it is fetched away from my lodging by gentlemen of your city, strangers of the Terra Firma,[17] worshipful merchants, ay, and senators too; who, ever since my arrival, have detained me to their uses, by their splendidous liberalities. And worthily; for what avails your rich man to have his magazines[18] stuffed with moscadelli,[19] or of the purest grape, when his physicians prescribe him, on pain of death, to drink nothing but water cocted [20] with aniseeds? O health! Health! The blessing of the rich! The riches of the poor! Who can

---

[9] **Tabarine** zany in a troupe of Italian actors [10] **fabulist** spinner of fables [11] **eat** ate [12] **several** separate [13] **scartoccios** paper containers [14] **oppilations** obstructions [15] **half-pe'rth** half-pennyworth [16] **canaglia** rabble [17] **Terra Firma** continental possessions of the Venetian State [18] **magazines** storehouses [19] **moscadelli** muscatel wine [20] **cocted** boiled

buy thee at too dear a rate, since there is no enjoying this world without thee? Be not then so sparing of your purses, honorable gentlemen, as to abridge the natural course of life——"

PEREGRINE. You see his end?

SIR POLITIC. Ay, is't not good?

VOLPONE. "For when a humid flux, or catarrh, by the mutability of air, falls from your head into an arm, or shoulder, or any other part; take you a ducat, or your chequìn of gold, and apply to the place affected; see what good effect it can work. No, no, 'tis this blessed *unguento*, this rare extraction, that hath only power to disperse all malignant humors,[21] that proceed either of hot, cold, moist, or windy causes——"

PEREGRINE. I would he had put in dry, too.

SIR POLITIC. Pray you observe.

VOLPONE. "To fortify the most indigest and crude[22] stomach, ay, were it of one that, through extreme weakness, vomited blood, applying only a warm napkin to the place, after the unction[23] and fricace;[24] for the *vertigine*[25] in the head, putting but a drop into your nostrils, likewise behind the ears, a most sovereign and approved remedy; the *mal caduco*,[26] cramps, convulsions, paralyses, epilepsies, *tremor cordia*,[27] retired nerves,[28] ill vapors of the spleen, stoppings[29] of the liver, the stone,[30] the strangury,[31] *hernia ventosa*,[32] *iliaca passio*;[33] stops a *dysenteria* immediately; easeth the torsion[34] of the small guts; and cures *melancholia hypocondriaca*, being taken and applied, according to my printed receipt. (*Pointing to his bill and his glass.*) For this is the physician, this the medicine; this counsels, this cures; this gives the direction, this works the effect; and, in sum, both together may be termed an abstract of the theoric and practic in the Aesculapian art.[35] 'Twill cost you eight crowns.—And, Zan Fritada, pray thee sing a verse extempore in honor of it."

SIR POLITIC. How do you like him, sir?

PEREGRINE. Most strangely, I!

---

[21] **humors** body fluids [22] **crude** queasy [23] **unction** anointing [24] **fricace** massage [25] **vertigine** vertigo [26] **mal caduco** falling sickness, *i.e.*, epilepsy [27] **tremor cordia** palpitations of the heart [28] **retired nerves** shrunken sinews [29] **stoppings** obstructions [30] **stone** *i.e.*, kidney stone, etc. [31] **strangury** painful urination [32] **hernia ventosa** gassy tumor [33] **iliaca passio** intestinal cramp [34] **torsion** convulsion [35] **Aesculapian art** medicine

SIR POLITIC. Is not his language rare?
PEREGRINE.   But[36] alchemy,
I never heard the like; or Broughton's books.[37]

SONG.

"Had old Hippocrates or Galen,[38]
 That to their books put med'cines all in,
 But known this secret, they had never—
 Of which they will be guilty ever—
 Been murderers of so much paper,
 Or wasted many a hurtless taper.
 No Indian drug had e'er been famèd,
 Tobacco, sassafras[39] not namèd;
 Ne[40] yet of guacum[41] one small stick, sir,
 Nor Raymund Lully's great elixir.[42]
 Ne had been known the Danish Gonswart,[43]
 Or Paracelsus,[44] with his long-sword."

PEREGRINE. All this yet will not do; eight crowns is high.
VOLPONE. "No more.—Gentlemen, if I had but time to discourse to you the miraculous effects of this my oil, sur-named *oglio del Scoto;* with the countless catalogue of those I have cured of th' aforesaid and many more diseases; the patents and privileges of all the princes and common-wealths of Christendom; or but the depositions of those that appeared on my part, before the signory of the *Sanità*[45] and most learned college of physicians; where I was authorized, upon notice taken of the admirable virtues of my medicaments, and mine own excellency in matter of rare and unknown secrets, not only to disperse them pub-licly in this famous city, but in all the territories that hap-pily joy under the government of the most pious and mag-nificent states of Italy. But may some other gallant fellow say, 'O, there be divers[46] that make profession to have as good and as experimented receipts[47] as yours.' Indeed,

[36] But except for   [37] Broughton's books abstruse works of rab-binical scholarship   [38] Hippocrates or Galen the two most re-nowned physicians of antiquity   [39] Tobacco, sassafras both believed to have medicinal properties   [40] Ne Nor   [41] guacum medicinal bark   [42] Raymund Lully mediaeval alchemist and physician popularly credited with having discovered the elixir of life   [43] Gonswart unidentified   [44] Paracelsus German al-chemist and physician supposed to have hidden his remedies in the hilt of his sword   [45] signory . . . Sanità Venetian medical board   [46] divers many   [47] experimented receipts tested for-mulas

very many have assayed, like apes, in imitation of that which is really and essentially in me, to make of this oil; bestowed great cost in furnaces, stills, alembics, continual fires, and preparation of the ingredients,—as indeed there goes to it six hundred several simples,[48] besides some quantity of human fat, for the conglutination, which we buy of the anatomists—but when these practitioners come to the last decoction: blow, blow, puff, puff, and all flies in *fumo.*[49] Ha, ha, ha! Poor wretches! I rather pity their folly and indiscretion than their loss of time and money; for those may be recovered by industry, but to be a fool born is a disease incurable. For myself, I always from my youth have endeavored to get the rarest secrets, and book them, either in exchange or for money. I spared nor cost nor labor, where anything was worthy to be learned. And gentlemen, honorable gentlemen, I will undertake, by virtue of chemical art, out of the honorable hat that covers your head, to extract the four elements: that is to say, the fire, air, water, and earth, and return you your felt without burn or stain. For whilst others have been at the balloo,[50] I have been at my book; and am now past the craggy paths of study, and come to the flowery plains of honor and reputation."

SIR POLITIC. I do assure you, sir, that is his aim.

VOLPONE. "But to our price———"

PEREGRINE.   And that withal, Sir Poll.

VOLPONE. "You all know, honorable gentlemen, I never valued this *ampulla,* or vial, at less than eight crowns; but for this time, I am content to be deprived of it for six. Six crowns is the price, and less, in courtesy, I know you cannot offer me. Take it or leave it, howsoever, both it and I am at your service. I ask you not as the value of the thing, for then I should demand of you a thousand crowns; so the Cardinals Montalto, Farnese, the Great Duke of Tuscany, my gossip,[51] with divers other princes, have given me, but I despise money. Only to show my affection to you, honorable gentlemen, and your illustrious state here, I have neglected the messages of these princes, mine own offices; framed my journey hither only to present you with the fruits of my travels.—Tune your voices once more to the touch of your instruments, and give the honorable assembly some delightful recreation."

PEREGRINE. What monstrous and most painful circumstance

[48] **simples** medicinal herbs   [49] **fumo** smoke   [50] **balloo** Venetian game of ball   [51] **gossip** godfather

Is here, to get some three or four *gazets*,[52]
Some threepence i' the whole! For that 'twill come to.

Song.

"You that would last long, list to my song,
   Make no more coil,[53] but buy of this oil.
Would you be ever fair and young?
Stout of teeth and strong of tongue?
Tart[54] of palate? Quick of ear?
Sharp of sight? Of nostril clear?
Moist of hand and light of foot?
Or I will come nearer to't—
Would you live free from all diseases?
Do the act your mistress pleases,
Yet fright all aches[55] from your bones?
Here's a med'cine for the nones." [56]

VOLPONE. "Well, I am in a humor at this time to make
a present of the small quantity my coffer contains; to the
rich, in courtesy, and to the poor, for God's sake. Wherefore now mark: I asked you six crowns, and six crowns, at
other times, you have paid me. You shall not give me six
crowns, nor five, nor four, nor three, nor two, nor one; nor
half a ducat; no, nor a *moccenigo!* [57] Six—pence it will
cost you, or six hundred pound—expect no lower price, for
by the banner of my front, I will not bate a *bagatine*;[57] that
I will have, only, a pledge of your loves, to carry something
from amongst you, to show I am not contemned by you.
Therefore now, toss your handkerchiefs, cheerfully, cheerfully; and be advertised that the first heroic spirit that
deigns to grace me with a handkerchief, I will give it a
little remembrance of something beside, shall please it
better than if I had presented it with a double pistolet." [58]

PEREGRINE. Will you be that heroic spark,[59] Sir Poll?
(CELIA, *at the window, throws down her handkerchief.*)
O, see, the window has prevented you!

VOLPONE. "Lady, I kiss your bounty; and for this timely
grace you have done your poor Scoto of Mantua, I will
return you, over and above my oil, a secret of that high
and inestimable nature, shall make you forever enamored
on that minute wherein your eye first descended on so

[52] gazets Venetian small change [53] coil ado [54] tart keen
[55] aches pronounced "aitches" [56] for . . . nones for the purpose [57] moccenigo, bagatine small Italian coins [58] pistolet
Spanish gold piece [59] spark young gentleman

mean, yet not altogether to be despised, an object. Here
is a powder concealed in this paper, of which, if I should
speak to the worth, nine thousand volumes were but as one
page, that page as a line, that line as a word; so short is
this pilgrimage of man, which some call life, to the express-
ing of it. Would I reflect on the price? Why, the whole
world were but as an empire, that empire as a province,
that province as a bank, that bank as a private purse, to the
purchase of it. I will only tell you: it is the powder that
made Venus a goddess,—given her by Apollo—that kept
her perpetually young, cleared her wrinkles, firmed her
gums, filled her skin, colored her hair; from her derived [60]
to Helen, and at the sack of Troy unfortunately lost; till
now, in this our age, it was as happily recovered by a
studious antiquary, out of some ruins of Asia; who sent a
moiety[61] of it to the court of France—but much sophisticated [62]—wherewith the ladies there now color their hair.
The rest, at this present, remains with me; extracted to a
quintessence, so that, wherever it but touches, in youth it
perpetually preserves, in age restores the complexion; seats
your teeth, did they dance like virginal jacks,[63] firm as a
wall; makes them white as ivory, that were black as——"

[*Enter* Corvino.]

Corvino. Spite o' the devil, and my shame! Come down,
here,
Come down! No house but mine to make your scene?
Signor Flaminio, will you down, sir? Down?
What, is my wife your *Franciscina*, sir?
No windows on the whole Piazza here,
To make your properties, but mine? But mine?
(*He beats away* Volpone, Mosca, Nano, *and* Grege.)
Heart! Ere tomorrow I shall be new christened,
And called the *Pantalone di Bisognosi*
About the town.
        Peregrine. What should this mean, Sir Poll?
10   Sir Politic. Some trick of state, believe it. I will home.

[60] **derived** conveyed   [61] **moiety** share   [62] **sophisticated** adulter-
ated   [63] **virginal jacks** stiff pieces of wood in which the quills
are fixed that pluck the strings of the virginal, or spinet. But
Volpone may only be referring to the keys.   2 **scene** stage
3 **Flaminio** well-known Italian actor   4 **Franciscina** the flirta-
tious maid-servant of the *commedia dell' arte*   8 **Pantalone di
Bisognosi** the jealous old husband and cuckold of the *commedia
dell' arte*

PEREGRINE. It may be some design on you.
SIR POLITIC.   I know not.
I'll stand upon my guard.
   PEREGRINE.   It is your best, sir.
   SIR POLITIC. This three weeks, all my advices, all my let-
      ters,
They have been intercepted.
   PEREGRINE.   Indeed, sir?
Best have a care.
   SIR POLITIC.   Nay, so I will.
   PEREGRINE.   This knight,
I may not lose him, for my mirth, till night.

                                      [*Exeunt*.]

                        SCENE TWO

                        [*A street*]

              [*Enter* VOLPONE *and* MOSCA.]

   VOLPONE. O, I am wounded!
   MOSCA.   Where, sir?
   VOLPONE.   Not without;
Those blows were nothing. I could bear them ever.
But angry Cupid, bolting from her eyes,
Hath shot himself into me like a flame;
Where now he flings about his burning heat,
As in a furnace an ambitious fire,
Whose vent is stopped. The fight is all within me.
I cannot live, except thou help me, Mosca.
My liver melts, and I, without the hope
Of some soft air from her refreshing breath,   10
Am but a heap of cinders.
   MOSCA.   'Las, good sir,
Would you had never seen her!
   VOLPONE.   Nay, would thou
Hadst never told me of her!
   MOSCA.   Sir, 'tis true;
I do confess I was unfortunate,
And you unhappy; but I'm bound in conscience,
No less than duty, to effect my best
To your release of torment, and I will, sir.
   VOLPONE. Dear Mosca, shall I hope?

6 **ambitious** swelling   9 **liver** supposed to be the seat of
passion

MOSCA.   Sir, more than dear,
I will not bid you to despair of aught
Within a human compass.
20   VOLPONE.   O, there spoke
My better angel. Mosca, take my keys,
Gold, plate, and jewels—all's at thy devotion.
Employ them how thou wilt; nay, coin me, too—
So thou in this but crown my longings, Mosca.
       MOSCA. Use but your patience.
       VOLPONE.   So I have.
       MOSCA.   I doubt not
To bring success to your desires.
       VOLPONE.   Nay, then,
I not repent me of my late disguise.
       MOSCA. If you can horn him, sir, you need not.
       VOLPONE.   True.
Besides, I never meant him for my heir.
30 Is not the color o' my beard and eyebrows
To make me known?
       MOSCA.   No jot.
       VOLPONE.   I did it well.
       MOSCA. So well, would I could follow you in mine,
With half the happiness! And yet I would
Escape your epilogue.
       VOLPONE.   But were they gulled
With a belief that I was Scoto?
       MOSCA.   Sir,
Scoto himself could hardly have distinguished!
I have not time to flatter you now, we'll part;
And as I prosper, so applaud my art.   [Exeunt.]

SCENE THREE

[Corvino's house]

[Enter CORVINO dragging in CELIA.]

    CORVINO. Death of mine honor, with the city's fool!
A juggling, tooth-drawing, prating mountebank!
And at a public window! Where, whilst he,
With his strained action, and his dole of faces,
To his drug-lecture draws your itching ears,

22 at . . . devotion at thy disposal   28 horn him furnish him
with horns, make him a cuckold   34 your epilogue i.e., the
beating   4 dole of faces repertory of grimaces

A crew of old, unmarried, noted lechers
Stood leering up like satyrs; and you smile
Most graciously, and fan your favors forth,
To give your hot spectators satisfaction!
What, was your mountebank their call? Their whistle?   10
Or were y' enamored on his copper rings?
His saffron jewel with the toad-stone in't?
Or his embroidered suit, with the cope-stitch,
Made of a hearse-cloth? Or his old tilt-feather?
Or his starched beard? Well, you shall have him, yes!
He shall come home, and minister unto you
The fricace for the mother. Or, let me see,
I think you'd rather mount; would you not mount?
Why, if you'll mount, you may; yes, truly, you may!
And so you may be seen, down to th' foot.   20
Get you a cittern, Lady Vanity,
And be a dealer with the virtuous man;
Make one. I'll but protest myself a cuckold,
And save your dowry. I am a Dutchman, I!
For if you thought me an Italian,
You would be damned ere you did this, you whore!
Thou'dst tremble to imagine that the murder
Of father, mother, brother, all thy race,
Should follow, as the subject of my justice!
    CELIA. Good sir, have patience.
    CORVINO.   What couldst thou propose 30
Less to thyself than, in this heat of wrath,
And stung with my dishonor, I should strike
This steel into thee, with as many stabs
As thou wert gazed upon with goatish eyes?
    CELIA. Alas, sir, be appeased! I could not think
My being at the window should more now
Move your impatience than at other times.
    CORVINO. No? Not to seek and entertain a parley
With a known knave, before a multitude!
You were an actor, with your handkerchief,   40
Which he most sweetly kissed in the receipt,

---

11 **rings** commonly worn by jugglers   12 **toad-stone** piece of
stone supposedly extracted from the head of a toad and worn
as a charm   13 **cope-stitch** stitch used in embroidering ceremonial robes   14 **tilt-feather** feather worn at tilting, or jousting,
perhaps in a helmet   15 **starched beard** fashionable in London
at this time   17 **mother** hysteria   21 **cittern** zither **Lady
Vanity** allegorical character in the early English morality plays
22 **dealer** prostitute **virtuous man** virtuoso

And might, no doubt, return it with a letter,
And 'point the place where you might meet—your sister's,
Your mother's, or your aunt's might serve the turn.
   CELIA. Why, dear sir, when do I make these excuses,
Or ever stir abroad, but to the church?
And that so seldom——
   CORVINO.   Well, it shall be less;
And thy restraint before was liberty
To what I now decree. And therefore mark me:
50 First, I will have this bawdy light dammed up;
And till't be done, some two or three yards off,
I'll chalk a line, o'er which if thou but chance
To set thy desp'rate foot, more hell, more horror,
More wild remorseless rage shall seize on thee
Than on a conjuror that had heedless left
His circle's safety ere his devil was laid.
Then, here's a lock which I will hang upon thee;
And, now I think on't, I will keep thee backwards;
Thy lodging shall be backwards, thy walks backwards,
60 Thy prospect—all be backwards, and no pleasure
That thou shalt know. but backwards. Nay, since you force
My honest nature, know it is your own
Being too open, makes me use you thus;
Since you will not contain your subtle nostrils
In a sweet room, but they must snuff the air
Of rank and sweaty passengers.   (*Knock within.*)
   One knocks.
Away, and be not seen, pain of thy life;
Not look toward the window; if thou dost—
Nay, stay, hear this—let me not prosper, whore,
70 But I will make thee an anatomy,
Dissect thee mine own self, and read a lecture
Upon thee to the city, and in public.
Away!—   [*Exit* CELIA.]

[*Enter* SERVITORE.]
      Who's there?
   SERVITORE.   'Tis Signor Mosca, sir.
   CORVINO. Let him come in. [*Exit* SERVITORE.] His
    master's dead! There's yet
Some good to help the bad.

---

56 circle *i.e.*, charmed circle, within which the conjuror was
safe from the devil he had raised up   **laid** exorcised   **57 lock**
girdle of chastity   **66 passengers** passersby   **70 make . . .
anatomy** use you as a demonstration cadaver

[*Enter* MOSCA.]

My Mosca, welcome!
I guess your news.

MOSCA.   I fear you cannot, sir.

CORVINO. Is't not his death?

MOSCA.   Rather the contrary.

CORVINO. Not his recovery?

MOSCA.   Yes, sir.

CORVINO.   I am cursed,
I am bewitched, my crosses meet to vex me!
How? How? How? How?

MOSCA.   Why, sir, with Scoto's oil!   80
Corbaccio and Voltore brought of it
Whilst I was busy in an inner room——

CORVINO. Death! That damned mountebank! But for the
    law
Now, I could kill the rascal; 't cannot be
His oil should have that virtue. Ha' not I
Known him, a common rogue, come fiddling in
To th' *osteria*, with a tumbling whore,
And, when he has done all his forced tricks, been glad
Of a poor spoonful of dead wine, with flies in't?
It cannot be. All his ingredients   90
Are a sheep's gall, a roasted bitch's marrow,
Some few sod earwigs, pounded caterpillars,
A little capon's grease, and fasting spittle.
I know 'em to a dram.

MOSCA.   I know not, sir,
But some on't there they poured into his ears,
Some in his nostrils, and recovered him,
Applying but the fricace!

CORVINO.   Pox o' that fricace!

MOSCA. And since, to seem the more officious,
And flatt'ring of his health, there they have had,
At èxtreme fees, the college of physicians   100
Consulting on him, how they might restore him;
Where one would have a cataplasm of spices,
Another a flayed ape clapped to his breast,
A third would ha' it a dog, a fourth an oil,
With wild cats' skins; at last, they all resolved
That, to preserve him, was no other means
But some young woman must be straight sought out,

85 **virtue** efficacy 87 **osteria** inn **tumbling** somersaulting
92 **sod** boiled 93 **fasting spittle** saliva from one who has been
fasting 98 **officious** zealous 102 **cataplasm** poultice

Lusty and full of juice, to sleep by him.
And to this service, most unhappily,
110 And most unwillingly, am I now employed;
Which here I thought to pre-acquaint you with,
For your advice, since it concerns you most,
Because I would not do that thing might cross
Your ends, on whom I have my whole dependence, sir.
Yet, if I do it not, they may delate
My slackness to my patron, work me out
Of his opinion; and there all your hopes,
Ventures, or whatsoever, are all frustrate.
I do but tell you, sir. Besides, they are all
120 Now striving who shall first present him. Therefore—
I could entreat you, briefly, conclude somewhat;
Prevent 'em if you can!
    Corvino.   Death to my hopes,
This is my villainous fortune! Best to hire
Some common courtesan.
    Mosca.   Ay, I thought on that, sir;
But they are all so subtle, full of art;
And age again doting and flexible,
So as—I cannot tell—we may perchance
Light on a quean may cheat us all.
    Corvino.   'Tis true.
    Mosca. No, no. It must be one that has no tricks, sir,
130 Some simple thing, a creature made unto it;
Some wench you may command. Ha' you no kinswoman?
God's so'—Think, think, think, think, think, think, think,
    sir.
One o' the doctors offered there his daughter.
    Corvino. How!
    Mosca.   Yes, Signor Lupo, the physician.
    Corvino. His daughter!
    Mosca.   And a virgin, sir. Why, alas,
He knows the state of's body, what it is;
That nought can warm his blood, sir, but a fever;
Nor any incantation raise his spirit—
A long forgetfulness hath seized that part.
140 Besides, sir, who shall know it? Some one or two—
    Corvino. I pray thee give me leave. [*Walks aside.*] —If
    any man
But I had had this luck—The thing in'tself,
I know, is nothing—Wherefore should not I
As well command my blood and my affections

115 **delate** accuse   128 **quean** harlot

As this dull doctor? In the point of honor,
The cases are all one, of wife and daughter.
   MOSCA. [*Aside.*] —I hear him coming.
   CORVINO.   She shall do't. 'Tis done.
'Slight! If this doctor, who is not engaged,
Unless 't be for his counsel, which is nothing,
Offer his daughter, what should I, that am   **150**
So deeply in? I will prevent him. Wretch!
Covetous wretch!—Mosca, I have determined.
   MOSCA. How, sir?
   CORVINO.   We'll make all sure. The party you wot
   of
Shall be mine own wife, Mosca.
   MOSCA.   Sir, the thing,
But that I would not seem to counsel you,
I should have motioned to you at the first;
And, make your count, you have cut all their throats.
Why, 'tis directly taking a possession!
And in his next fit, we may let him go.
'Tis but to pull the pillow from his head,   **160**
And he is throttled; 't had been done before,
But for your scrupulous doubts.
   CORVINO.   Ay, a plague on't,
My conscience fools my wit! Well, I'll be brief,
And so be thou, lest they should be before us.
Go home, prepare him, tell him with what zeal
And willingness I do it. Swear it was
On the first hearing—as thou mayst do, truly—
Mine own free motion.
   MOSCA.   Sir, I warrant you,
I'll so possess him with it, that the rest
Of his starved clients shall be banished all,   **170**
And only you received. But come not, sir,
Until I send, for I have something else
To ripen for your good; you must not know't.
   CORVINO. But do not you forget to send now.
   MOSCA.   Fear not.
                                [*Exit.*]
   CORVINO. Where are you, wife? My Celia! Wife!

            [*Re-enter* CELIA.]

                          What, blubbering?
Come, dry those tears. I think thou thought'st me in
   earnest!

147 **coming** yielding   151 **prevent** anticipate   153 **wot** know
156 **motioned** proposed

Ha! By this light, I talked so but to try thee.
Methinks the lightness of the occasion
Should ha' confirmed thee. Come, I am not jealous.
     CELIA. No?
180   CORVINO.   Faith I am not, I, nor never was;
It is a poor, unprofitable humor.
Do not I know, if women have a will,
They'll do 'gainst all the watches o' the world?
And that the fiercest spies are tamed with gold?
Tut, I am confident in thee, thou shalt see't;
And see, I'll give thee cause, too, to believe it.
Come kiss me. Go, and make thee ready straight
In all thy best attire, thy choicest jewels,
Put 'em all on, and, with 'em, thy best looks.
We are invited to a solemn feast
At old Volpone's, where it shall appear
How far I am free from jealousy or fear.   [*Exeunt.*]

Act Three

SCENE ONE

[*A street*]

[*Enter* MOSCA.]

     MOSCA. I fear I shall begin to grow in love
With my dear self, and my most prosp'rous parts,
They do so spring and burgeon! I can feel
A whimsy i' my blood; I know not how,
Success hath made me wanton. I could skip
Out of my skin now, like a subtle snake,
I am so limber. O! Your parasite
Is a most precious thing, dropped from above,
Not bred 'mongst clods and clodpolls here on earth.
10 I muse the mystery was not made a science,
It is so liberally professed! Almost
All the wise world is little else, in nature,
But parasites or sub-parasites. And yet
I mean not those that have your bare town-art,
To know who's fit to feed 'em; have no house,

181 **humor** disposition   183 **do betray their husbands   watches**
guard   2 **parts** talents   3 **spring** sprout   9 **clodpolls** numb-
skulls   10 **mystery** art   11 **liberally professed** widely practiced

No family, no care, and therefore mold
Tales for men's ears, to bait that sense; or get
Kitchen-invention, and some stale receipts
To please the belly and the groin; nor those,
With their court-dog tricks, that can fawn and fleer,   20
Make their revènue out of legs and faces,
Echo my lord, and lick away a moth;
But your fine, elegant rascal, that can rise
And stoop, almost together, like an arrow;
Shoot through the air as nimbly as a star;
Turn short as doth a swallow; and be here,
And there, and here, and yonder, all at once;
Present to any humor all occasion,
And change a visor swifter than a thought!
This is the creature had the art born with him;   30
Toils not to learn it, but doth practise it
Out of most excellent nature; and such sparks
Are the true parasites, others but their zanies.

[*Enter* BONARIO.]

Who's this? Bonario, old Corbaccio's son?
The person I was bound to seek.—Fair sir,
You are happ'ly met.
    BONARIO.   That cannot be by thee.
    MOSCA. Why, sir?
    BONARIO.   Nay, pray thee know thy way, and
    leave me.
I would be loath to interchange discourse
With such a mate as thou art.
    MOSCA.   Courteous sir,
Scorn not my poverty.
    BONARIO.   Not I, by heaven!
But thou shalt give me leave to hate thy baseness.   40
    MOSCA. Baseness?
    BONARIO.   Ay, answer me, is not thy sloth
Sufficient argument? Thy flattery?
Thy means of feeding?
    MOSCA.   Heaven be good to me!
These imputations are too common, sir,
And eas'ly stuck on virtue when she's poor;

18 **Kitchen-invention** ingenuity in cookery   **receipts** recipes
21 **legs** bows   22 **lick . . . moth** *i.e.,* from the lord's person
28 **Present . . . occasion** find ways of gratifying every whim
32 **Out . . . nature** from natural talent   **sparks** clever fellows
33 **zanies** mimics   39 **mate** base fellow

You are unequal to me, and howe'er
Your sentence may be righteous, yet you are not,
That, ere you know me, thus proceed in censure.
50 St. Mark bear witness 'gainst you, 'tis inhuman!
    BONARIO. [*Aside.*] —What! Does he weep? The sign is
        soft and good.
I do repent me that I was so harsh.
    MOSCA. 'Tis true that, swayed by strong necessity,
I am enforced to eat my careful bread
With too much obsequy. 'Tis true, beside,
That I am fain to spin mine own poor raiment
Out of my mere observance, being not born
To a free fortune. But that I have done
Base offices, in rending friends asunder,
60 Dividing families, betraying counsels,
Whispering false lies, or mining men with praises,
Trained their credulity with perjuries,
Corrupted chastity, or am in love
With mine own tender ease; but would not rather
Prove the most rugged and laborious course
That might redeem my present estimation,
Let me here perish, in all hope of goodness!
    BONARIO. [*Aside.*] This cannot be a personated pas-
        sion.—
I was to blame, so to mistake thy nature.
70 Pray thee forgive me, and speak out thy business.
    MOSCA. Sir, it concerns you; and though I may seem
At first to make a main offence in manners,
And in my gratitude unto my master,
Yet for the pure love which I bear all right,
And hatred of the wrong, I must reveal it.
This very hour your father is in purpose
To disinherit you——
    BONARIO.   How!
    MOSCA.   And thrust you forth,
As a mere stranger to his blood; 'tis true, sir!
The work no way engageth me, but as
80 I claim an interest in the general state
Of goodness and true virtue, which I hear

---

47 **unequal** unjust   54 **careful** attended by sorrow and anxiety
55 **obsequy** obsequiousness 57 **observance** dutiful service 61
mining undermining 62 **Trained** ensnared 65 **prove** undergo
66 **estimation** reputation 68 **personated** counterfeited 72
main very great 78 **mere** absolute

T' abound in you; and for which mere respect,
Without a second aim, sir, I have done it.
  BONARIO. This tale hath lost thee much of the late trust
Thou hadst with me; it is impossible.
I know not how to lend it any thought,
My father should be so unnatural.
  MOSCA. It is a confidence that well becomes
Your piety; and formed, no doubt, it is
From your own simple innocence; which makes   90
Your wrong more monstrous and abhorred. But, sir,
I now will tell you more: this very minute
It is, or will be, doing; and if you
Shall be but pleased to go with me, I'll bring you—
I dare not say where you shall see—but where
Your ear shall be a witness of the deed;
Hear yourself written bastard, and professed
The common issue of the earth.
  BONARIO.   I'm 'mazed!
  MOSCA. Sir, if I do it not, draw your just sword,
And score your vengeance on my front and face;   100
Mark me your villain. You have too much wrong,
And I do suffer for you, sir. My heart
Weeps blood in anguish——
  BONARIO.   Lead. I follow thee.
                                [*Exeunt.*]

SCENE TWO

[*Volpone's house*]

[*Enter* VOLPONE.]

VOLPONE. Mosca stays long, methinks.—Bring forth
    your sports,
And help to make the wretched time more sweet.

[*Enter* NANO, ANDROGYNO, *and* CASTRONE.]

NANO. "Dwarf, fool, and eunuch, well met here we be.
A question it were now, whether of us three,
Being all the known delicates of a rich man,
In pleasing him, claim the precedency can?"

82 **for . . . respect** from this consideration alone 89 **piety**
filial affection 97 **professed** proclaimed 98 **The . . . earth**
a fellow of unknown origins, a nobody 100 **front** forehead
4 **whether** which 5 **delicates** pets, favorites

CASTRONE. "I claim for myself."
ANDROGYNO.   "And so doth the fool."
NANO. " 'Tis foolish indeed. Let me set you both to
    school:
First, for your dwarf, he's little and witty,
10 And everything, as it is little, is pretty;
Else why do men say to a creature of my shape,
So soon as they see him, 'It's a pretty little ape'?
And why a pretty ape, but for pleasing imitation
Of greater men's action, in a ridiculous fashion?
Beside, this feat body of mine doth not crave
Half the meat, drink, and cloth one of your bulks will have.
Admit your fool's face be the mother of laughter,
Yet, for his brain, it must always come after;
And though that do feed him, it's a pitiful case,
20 His body is beholden to such a bad face."

                                       (*One knocks.*)
VOLPONE. Who's there? My couch! Away! Look!
    Nano, see!   [*Exeunt* ANDROGYNO *and* CASTRONE.]
Give me my caps first—go, inquire.   [*Exit* NANO.]
    Now, Cupid
Send it be Mosca, and with fair return!
  NANO. It is the beauteous Madam—
VOLPONE.   Wouldbe—is it?
NANO. The same.
VOLPONE.   Now torment on me! Squire her in;
For she will enter, or dwell here forever.
Nay, quickly, that my fit were past. I fear
A second hell, too, that my loathing this
Will quite expel my appetite to the other.
30 Would she were taking now her tedious leave.
Lord, how it threats me, what I am to suffer!

         [*Re-enter* NANO *with* LADY WOULDBE.]

  LADY WOULDBE. I thank you, good sir. Pray you signify
Unto your patron I am here.—This band
Shows not my neck enough.—I trouble you, sir;
Let me request you bid one of my women
Come hither to me. In good faith, I am dressed
Most favorably today! It is no matter;
'Tis well enough.

---

15 **feat** graceful   23 **Send** grant   28 **this** *i.e.,* Lady Wouldbe
29 **the other** *i.e.,* Celia   33 **band** ruff

[*Enter* 1ST WOMAN.]
                    Look, see these petulant things!
How they have done this!
     VOLPONE. [*Aside.*]   —I do feel the fever
Ent'ring in at mine ears. O for a charm   40
To fright it hence!
     LADY WOULDBE. Come nearer. Is this curl
In his right place, or this? Why is this higher
Than all the rest? You ha' not washed your eyes yet!
Or do they not stand even i' your head?
Where is your fellow? Call her.   [*Exit* 1ST WOMAN.]
     NANO.   —Now, St. Mark
Deliver us! Anon she'll beat her women,
Because her nose is red.

     [*Re-enter* 1ST WOMAN *with* 2ND WOMAN.]

     LADY WOULDBE.   I pray you, view
This tire, forsooth; are all things apt, or no?
     1ST WOMAN. One hair a little here sticks out, forsooth.
     LADY WOULDBE. Does't so, forsooth? And where was your 50
          dear sight,
When it did so, forsooth? What now! Bird-eyed?
And you too? Pray you both approach and mend it.
Now, by that light, I muse you're not ashamed!
I, that have preached these things so oft unto you,
Read you the principles, argued all the grounds,
Disputed every fitness, every grace,
Called you to counsel of so frequent dressings——
     NANO. [*Aside.*] —More carefully than of your fame or
          honor.
     LADY WOULDBE. Made you acquainted what an ample
          dowry
The knowledge of these things would be unto you,   60
Able alone to get you noble husbands
At your return; and you thus to neglect it!
Besides, you seeing what a curious nation
Th' Italians are, what will they say of me?
"The English lady cannot dress herself."
Here's a fine imputation to our country!
Well, go your ways, and stay i' the next room.
This fucus was too coarse, too; it's no matter.—
Good sir, you'll give 'em entertainment?
                         [*Exit* NANO *with* WOMEN.]

46 **anon** now   48 **tire** headdress   53 **muse** wonder   63 **curious**
fastidious   68 **fucus** cosmetic   69 **give . . . entertainment** pro-
vide for them

VOLPONE. —The storm comes toward me.

70 LADY WOULDBE. How does my Volp?

VOLPONE. Troubled with noise, I cannot sleep; I dreamt
That a strange fury entered now my house,
And with the dreadful tempest of her breath
Did cleave my roof asunder.

LADY WOULDBE. Believe me, and I
Had the most fearful dream, could I remember't——

VOLPONE. [*Aside.*] —Out on my fate! I ha' giv'n her the occasion
How to torment me: she will tell me hers.

LADY WOULDBE. Methought the golden mediocrity,
Polite and delicate——

VOLPONE. O, if you do love me,
80 No more! I sweat and suffer at the mention
Of any dream. Feel how I tremble yet.

LADY WOULDBE. Alas, good soul! The passion of the heart.
Seed-pearl were good now, boiled with syrup of apples,
Tincture of gold, and coral, citron pills,
Your elecampane root, myrobalanes——

VOLPONE. [*Aside.*] —Ay me, I have ta'en a grasshopper by the wing!

LADY WOULDBE. Burnt silk and amber; you have muscadel
Good i' the house——

VOLPONE. You will not drink, and part?

LADY WOULDBE. No, fear not that. I doubt we shall not get
90 Some English saffron,—half a dram would serve—
Your sixteen cloves, a little musk, dried mints,
Bugloss, and barley-meal——

VOLPONE. [*Aside.*] —She's in again!
Before, I feigned diseases; now I have one.

LADY WOULDBE. And these applied with a right scarlet cloth.

VOLPONE. [*Aside.*] —Another flood of words! A very torrent!

LADY WOULDBE. Shall I, sir, make you a poultice?

VOLPONE. No, no, no!
I'm very well; you need prescribe no more.

LADY WOULDBE. I have a little studied physic; but now
I'm all for music, save, i' the forenoons,

---

82 passion . . . heart heartburn **83 Seed-pearl** the first in
a series of popular remedies prescribed by Lady Wouldbe

An hour or two for painting. I would have   100
A lady, indeed, t' have all, letters and arts,
Be able to discourse, to write, to paint;
But principal—as Plato holds—your music—
And so does wise Pythagoras, I take it—
Is your true rapture; when there is consent
In face, in voice, and clothes; and is, indeed,
Our sex's chiefest ornament.
  VOLPONE.   The poet
As old in time as Plato, and as knowing,
Says that your highest female grace is silence.
  LADY WOULDBE. Which o' your poets? Petrarch, or 110
  Tasso, or Dante?
Guarini? Ariosto? Aretine?
Cieco di Hadria? I have read them all.
  VOLPONE. [*Aside.*] —Is everything a cause to my de-
  struction?
  LADY WOULDBE. I think I ha' two or three of 'em about
  me.
  VOLPONE. [*Aside.*] —The sun, the sea, will sooner both
  stand still
Than her eternal tongue! Nothing can 'scape it.
  LADY WOULDBE. Here's *Pastor Fido*——
  VOLPONE. [*Aside.*]   —Profess obstinate silence,
That's now my safest.
  LADY WOULDBE. All our English writers,
I mean such as are happy in th' Italian,
Will deign to steal out of this author mainly,   120
Almost as much as from Montagnié.
He has so modern and facile a vein,
Fitting the time, and catching the court ear.
Your Petrarch is more passionate, yet he,
In days of sonnetting, trusted 'em with much.
Dante is hard, and few can understand him.
But, for a desperate wit, there's Aretine!

101 **have** know 105 **consent** harmony 110 **Petrarch** Lady
Wouldbe mentions most of the Italian poets famous in England during the Renaissance, and a minor writer, Luigi Groto,
known as Cieco di Hadria 117 **Pastor Fido** *The Faithful
Shepherd,* a pastoral play by Guarini, widely read and imitated
in England 119 **happy** fluent 121 **Montagnié** pronounced as
four syllables: Montaigne, the French essayist and skeptic 124
Petrarch . . . passionate Petrarch's best-known work was a
sequence of love sonnets 127 **desperate** outrageous **Aretine**
Aretino, author of a set of scurrilous sonnets written to ac-
company obscene drawings

Only his pictures are a little obscene——
You mark me not.
    VOLPONE.   Alas, my mind's perturbed.
130 LADY WOULDBE. Why, in such cases we must cure our-
       selves,
Make use of our philosophy——
    VOLPONE.   O 'y me!
    LADY WOULDBE. And as we find our passions do rebel,
Encounter 'em with reason, or divert 'em,
By giving scope unto some other humor
Of lesser danger; as, in politic bodies,
There's nothing more doth overwhelm the judgment
And clouds the understanding, than too much
Settling and fixing and, as 'twere, subsiding
Upon one object. For the incorporating
140 Of these same outward things into that part
Which we call mental, leaves some certain faeces
That stop the organs, and, as Plato says,
Assassinates our knowledge.
    VOLPONE. [*Aside*.]   —Now, the spirit
Of patience help me!
    LADY WOULDBE.   Come, in faith, I must
Visit you more a-days, and make you well;
Laugh and be lusty!
    VOLPONE. [*Aside*.] —My good angel save me!
    LADY WOULDBE. There was but one sole man in all the
       world
With whom I e'er could sympathize; and he
Would lie you often three, four hours together
150 To hear me speak; and be sometime so rapt,
As he would answer me quite from the purpose,
Like you, and you are like him, just. I'll discourse,
An't be but only, sir, to bring you asleep,
How we did spend our time and loves together,
For some six years.
    VOLPONE.   O, O, O, O, O, O!
    LADY WOULDBE. For we were *coaetanei*, and brought
       up——
    VOLPONE. Some power, some fate, some fortune rescue
       me!

                [*Enter* MOSCA.]

MOSCA. God save you, madam!
132-143 Lady Wouldbe offers a sample of her "philosophy"
141 faeces dregs   **149 lie you** lie   **156 coaetanei** of the same
age

LADY WOULDBE.   Good sir.
VOLPONE.   —Mosca! Welcome,
Welcome to my redemption.
MOSCA.   Why, sir?
VOLPONE.   —O,
Rid me of this my torture, quickly, there,   160
My madam with the everlasting voice!
The bells, in time of pestilence, ne'er made
Like noise, or were in that perpetual motion;
The cock-pit comes not near it. All my house,
But now, steamed like a bath with her thick breath;
A lawyer could not have been heard; nor scarce
Another woman, such a hail of words
She has let fall. For hell's sake, rid her hence.
    MOSCA. Has she presented?
VOLPONE.   O, I do not care!
I'll take her absence upon any price,   170
With any loss.
    MOSCA.   Madam——
LADY WOULDBE.   I ha' brought your patron
A toy, a cap here, of mine own work—
    MOSCA.   'Tis well.
I had forgot to tell you I saw your knight,
Where you'd little think it——
    LADY WOULDBE.   Where?
    MOSCA.   Marry,
Where yet, if you make haste, you may apprehend him;
Rowing upon the water in a gondole,
With the most cunning courtesan of Venice.
    LADY WOULDBE. Is't true?
MOSCA.   Pursue 'em, and believe your eyes.
Leave me to make your gift. [*Exit* LADY WOULDBE *hastily.*]
    —I knew 'twould take.
For lightly, they that use themselves most license   180
Are still most jealous.
VOLPONE.   Mosca, hearty thanks
For thy quick fiction, and delivery of me.
Now to my hopes, what sayst thou?

[*Re-enter* LADY WOULDBE.]

LADY WOULDBE.   But do you hear, sir?——
162 **bells . . . pestilence** during outbreaks of the plague in
London, the bells tolled almost continuously   164 **cock-pit**
cockfighting arena, notorious for the noise and confusion caused
by the betting   169 **presented** *i.e.*, her gift   180 **lightly** commonly

VOLPONE. —Again! I fear a paroxysm.
LADY WOULDBE.　　　　　　　　　Which way
Rowed they together?
　MOSCA.　　　　　　Toward the Rialto.
　LADY WOULDBE. I pray you lend me your dwarf.
　MOSCA.　　　　　　　　　I pray you take him.
　　　　　　　　　　　　　[*Exit* LADY WOULDBE.]
Your hopes, sir, are like happy blossoms, fair,
And promise timely fruit, if you will stay
But the maturing. Keep you at your couch;
190 Corbaccio will arrive straight, with the will.
When he is gone, I'll tell you more.　　　[*Exit.*]
　VOLPONE.　　　　　　　My blood,
My spirits are returned; I am alive!
And, like your wanton gamester at primero,
Whose thought had whispered to him, not go less,
Methinks I lie, and draw——for an encounter.
　　　　　　　[VOLPONE *withdraws to his couch.*]

SCENE THREE

[*The Same*]

[*Enter* MOSCA *with* BONARIO.]

　MOSCA. Sir, here concealed, you may hear all. But pray
　　you
Have patience, sir. (*One knocks.*) The same's your father
　knocks.
I am compelled to leave you.
　BONARIO.　　　　　Do so.—Yet
Cannot my thought imagine this a truth.

[MOSCA *leaves* BONARIO, *and admits* CORVINO,
followed by CELIA.]

　MOSCA. Death on me! You are come too soon, what
　　meant you?
Did not I say I would send?
　CORVINO.　　　　Yes, but I fear'd

---

185 **Rialto** great bridge over the Grand Canal　193 **wanton**
frolicsome　**primero** a fashionable card game. Volpone quibbles
on various technical terms of the game ("go less," "draw,"
"encounter") in reference to his design of seducing Celia.　1
here concealed Mosca hides Bonario behind a door opening
onto the stage

You might forget it, and then they prevent us.
 Mosca. [*Aside.*] —Prevent! Did e'er man haste so for his
  horns?
A courtier would not ply it so for a place.—
Well, now there's no helping it, stay here;   10
I'll presently return.
 Corvino.   Where are you, Celia?
You know not wherefore I have brought you hither?
 Celia. Not well, except you told me.
 Corvino.   Now I will:
Hark hither.   [*Whispers to her.*]
 Mosca. (*To* Bonario.) Sir, your father hath sent word
It will be half an hour ere he come.
And therefore, if you please to walk the while
Into that gallery—at the upper end
There are some books to entertain the time—
And I'll take care no man shall come unto you, sir.
 Bonario. Yes, I will stay there. [*Aside.*] —I do doubt 20
  this fellow.   [*Exit.*]
 Mosca. There, he is far enough; he can hear nothing;
And for his father, I can keep him off.
      [*Withdraws to* Volpone's *couch.*]
 Corvino. Nay, now there is no starting back, and there-
  fore
Resolve upon it; I have so decreed.
It must be done. Nor would I move't afore,
Because I would avoid all shifts and tricks
That might deny me.
 Celia.   Sir, let me beseech you,
Affect not these strange trials. If you doubt
My chastity, why, lock me up forever;
Make me the heir of darkness. Let me live   30
Where I may please your fears, if not your trust.
 Corvino. Believe it, I have no such humor, I.
All that I speak I mean; yet I am not mad,
Not horn-mad, see you? Go to, show yourself
Obedient, and a wife.
 Celia.   O heaven!
 Corvino.   I say it,
Do so.
 Celia. Was this the train?
 Corvino.   I've told you reasons:

7 they Corvino's imagined competitors for the honor of "cur-
ing" Volpone in this fashion 9 **place** position at court **11**
presently immediately 25 **move** propose 36 **train** trap

What the physicians have set down, how much
It may concern me, what my engagements are,
My means, and the necessity of those means
40 For my recovery. Wherefore, if you be
Loyal, and mine, be won, respect my venture.
CELIA. Before your honor?
CORVINO.   Honor! Tut, a breath;
There's no such thing in nature: a mere term
Invented to awe fools. What is my gold
The worse for touching? Clothes for being looked on?
Why, this 's no more. An old, decrepit wretch,
That has no sense, no sinew; takes his meat
With others' fingers; only knows to gape
When you do scald his gums; a voice, a shadow;
And what can this man hurt you?
50 CELIA.   Lord! What spirit
Is this hath entered him?
CORVINO.   And for your fame,
That's such a jig; as if I would go tell it,
Cry it on the Piazza! Who shall know it
But he that cannot speak it, and this fellow,
Whose lips are i' my pocket? Save yourself—
If you'll proclaim't, you may. I know no other
Should come to know it.
CELIA.   Are heaven and saints then **nothing?**
Will they be blind or stupid?
CORVINO.   How?
CELIA.   Good sir,
Be jealous still, emulate them; and think
60 What hate they burn with toward every sin.
CORVINO. I grant you. If I thought it were a sin,
I would not urge you. Should I offer this
To some young Frenchman, or hot Tuscan blood,
That had read Aretine, conned all his prints,
Knew every quirk within lust's labyrinth,
And were professed critic in lechery;
And I would look upon him, and applaud him—
This were a sin. But here 'tis contrary:
A pious work, mere charity, for physic,
70 And honest policy to assure mine own.
CELIA. O heaven! Canst thou suffer such a change?
VOLPONE. —Thou art mine honor, Mosca, and my pride,

---

52 jig farce   64 **Aretine . . . prints** the pornographic drawings for which Aretino wrote sonnets   65 **quirk** sudden twist
66 **critic** expert

My joy, my tickling, my delight! Go bring 'em.
 Mosca. Please you draw near, sir.
 Corvino.   Come on, what——
You will not be rebellious? By that light——
 Mosca. Sir, Signor Corvino, here, is come to see you.
 Volpone. Oh!
 Mosca.   And hearing of the consultation had,
So lately, for your health, is come to offer,
Or rather, sir, to prostitute——
 Corvino.   Thanks, sweet Mosca.
 Mosca. Freely, unasked, or unentreated——
 Corvino.   Well!   80
 Mosca. As the true, fervent instance of his love,
His own most fair and proper wife, the beauty
Only of price in Venice——
 Corvino.   'Tis well urged.
 Mosca. To be your comfortress, and to preserve you.
 Volpone. Alas, I'm past, already! Pray you thank him
For his good care and promptness; but for that,
'Tis a vain labor e'en to fight 'gainst heaven,
Applying fire to stone,—uh, uh, uh, uh!—
Making a dead leaf grow again. I take
His wishes gently, though; and you may tell him 90
What I've done for him. Marry, my state is hopeless!
Will him to pray for me, and t' use his fortune
With reverence when he comes to 't.
 Mosca.   Do you hear, sir?
Go to him with your wife.
 Corvino.   Heart of my father!
Wilt thou persist thus? Come, I pray thee, come.
Thou seest 'tis nothing, Celia. By this hand,
I shall grow violent. Come, do't, I say.
 Celia. Sir, kill me, rather. I will take down poison,
Eat burning coals, do anything——
 Corvino.   Be damned!
Heart, I will drag thee hence home by the hair, 100
Cry thee a strumpet through the streets, rip up
Thy mouth unto thine ears, and slit thy nose
Like a raw rochet—Do not tempt me, come!
Yield, I am loath—Death! I will buy some slave,
Whom I will kill, and bind thee to him alive,
And at my window hang you forth; devising
Some monstrous crime, which I, in capital letters,

82 **beauty . . . price** the only precious beauty 90 **gently**
courteously 103 **rochet** a fish

Will eat into thy flesh with aquafortis
And burning corsives, on this stubborn breast.
110 Now, by the blood thou has incensed, I'll do't!
    CELIA. Sir, what you please, you may; I am your martyr.
    CORVINO. Be not thus obstinate; I ha' not deserved it.
Think who it is entreats you. Pray thee, sweet—
Good faith, thou shalt have jewels, gowns, attires,
What thou wilt think, and ask. Do but go kiss him.
Or touch him but. For my sake—At my suit—
This once—No? Not? I shall remember this!
Will you disgrace me thus? D'you thirst my undoing?
    MOSCA. Nay, gentle lady, be advised.
    CORVINO.   No, no.
120 She has watched her time. God's precious, this is scurvy,
'Tis very scurvy; and you are——
    MOSCA.   Nay, good sir.
    CORVINO. An arrant locust, by heaven, a locust! Whore,
Crocodile, that hast thy tears prepared,
Expecting how thou'lt bid 'em flow——
    MOSCA.   Nay, pray you, sir,
She will consider.
    CELIA.   Would my life would serve
To satisfy!
    CORVINO. 'Sdeath! If she would but speak to him,
And save my reputation, 't were somewhat;
But spitefully to affect my utter ruin!
    MOSCA. Ay, now you've put your fortune in her hands.
130 Why, i'faith, it is her modesty; I must quit her.
If you were absent, she would be more coming;
I know it, and dare undertake for her.
What woman can before her husband? Pray you,
Let us depart, and leave her here.
    CORVINO.   Sweet Celia,
Thou mayst redeem all yet; I'll say no more.
If not, esteem yourself as lost. Nay, stay there.
                              [*Exit with* MOSCA.]
    CELIA. O God and his good angels! Whither, whither
Is shame fled human breasts, that with such ease,
Men dare put off your honors, and their own?
140 Is that which ever was a cause of life
Now placed beneath the basest circumstance,
And modesty an exile made, for money?
    VOLPONE. (*Leaps off from his couch.*) Ay, in Corvino,
    and such earth-fed minds,

108 aquafortis acid   **109 corsives** corrosives   **130 quit** acquit
131 coming submissive

That never tasted the true heav'n of love.
Assure thee, Celia, he that would sell thee
Only for hope of gain, and that uncertain,
He would have sold his part of paradise
For ready money, had he met a cope-man.
Why art thou 'mazed to see me thus revived?
Rather applaud thy beauty's miracle;   150
'Tis thy great work that hath, not now alone,
But sundry times raised me in several shapes,
And, but this morning, like a mountebank,
To see thee at thy window. Ay, before
I would have left my practice for thy love,
In varying figures I would have contended
With the blue Proteus, or the hornèd flood.
Now art thou welcome.
   CELIA.   Sir!
   VOLPONE.   Nay, fly me not.
Nor let thy false imagination
That I was bed-rid, make thee think I am so.   160
Thou shalt not find it. I am now as fresh,
As hot, as high, and in as jovial plight,
As when, in that so celebrated scene,
At recitation of our comedy
For entertainment of the great Valois,
I acted young Antinous; and attracted
The eyes and ears of all the ladies present,
T' admire each grateful gesture, note, and footing.

SONG.

   "Come, my Celia, let us prove,
   While we can, the sports of love.   170
   Time will not be ours forever,
   He at length our good will sever;
   Spend not then his gifts in vain.
   Suns that set may rise again;
   But if once we lose this light,
   'Tis with us perpetual night.
   Why should we defer our joys?
   Fame and rumor are but toys.

148 **cope-man** tradesman   115 **practice** scheming   156 **figures** shapes   157 **Proteus** sea-god who could transform himself into any shape   **hornèd flood** sea or river deity with horns   165 **Valois** Henry III of France, entertained with great splendor at Venice in 1574   166 **Antinous** favorite of the Emperor Hadrian, celebrated for his beauty   169 **prove** engage in   178 **toys** trifles

Cannot we delude the eyes
180   Of a few poor household spies?
Or his easier ears beguile,
Thus removèd by our wile?
'Tis no sin love's fruits to steal,
But the sweet thefts to reveal:
To be taken, to be seen,
These have crimes accounted been."

CELIA. Some sèrene blast me, or dire lightning strike
This my offending face!
    VOLPONE.   Why droops my Celia?
Thou hast, in place of a base husband, found
190 A worthy lover; use thy fortune well,
With secrecy and pleasure. See, behold
What thou art queen of, not in expectation—
As I feed others—but possessed and crowned.
See, here, a rope of pearl, and each more orient
Than that the brave Egyptian queen caroused—
Dissolve and drink 'em. See, a carbuncle,
May put out both the eyes of our St. Mark;
A diamond would have bought Lollia Paulina,
When she came in like starlight, hid with jewels
200 That were the spoils of provinces—take these
And wear, and lose 'em; yet remains an earring
To purchase them again, and this whole state.
A gem but worth a private patrimony
Is nothing; we will eat such at a meal.
The heads of parrots, tongues of nightingales,
The brains of peacocks, and of estriches,
Shall be our food; and, could we get the phoenix,
Though nature lost her kind, she were our dish.
    CELIA. Good sir, these things might move a mind af-
        fected
210 With such delights; but I, whose innocence
Is all I can think wealthy, or worth th' enjoying,
And which, once lost, I have nought to lose beyond it,

187 **sèrene** infectious vapor   194 **orient** pure   195 **brave**
splendid   **Egyptian queen** Cleopatra, who drank pearls dissolved in vinegar on a wager with Antony   198 **Lollia Paulina**
wife of a Roman governor who dressed magnificently in
plundered finery   207 **phoenix** mythical bird of which there
was never more than one at any time   208 **Though . . . kind**
Even if, by eating the phoenix, we were to render her species
("kind") extinct

Cannot be taken with these sensual baits.
If you have conscience——
    VOLPONE.   'Tis the beggar's virtue.
If thou hast wisdom, hear me, Celia.
Thy baths shall be the juice of gillyflowers,
Spirit of roses, and of violets,
The milk of unicorns, and panthers' breath
Gathered in bags, and mixed with Cretan wines.
Our drink shall be preparèd gold and amber,   220
Which we will take until my roof whirl round
With the vertigo; and my dwarf shall dance,
My eunuch sing, my fool make up the antic.
Whilst we, in changèd shapes, act Ovid's tales,
Thou like Europa now, and I like Jove,
Then I like Mars, and thou like Erycine;
So of the rest, till we have quite run through
And wearied all the fables of the gods.
Then will I have thee in more modern forms,
Attirèd like some sprightly dame of France,   230
Brave Tuscan lady, or proud Spanish beauty;
Sometimes unto the Persian Sophy's wife,
Or the Grand Signor's mistress; and for change,
To one of our most artful courtesans,
Or some quick Negro, or cold Russian.
And I will meet thee in as many shapes;
Where we may so transfuse our wand'ring souls
Out at our lips, and score up sums of pleasures,

> "That the curious shall not know
>   How to tell them as they flow;   240
>   And the envious, when they find
>   What their number is, be pined."

    CELIA. If you have ears that will be pierced, or eyes
That can be opened, a heart may be touched,
Or any part that yet sounds man about you;
If you have touch of holy saints, or heaven,
Do me the grace to let me 'scape. If not,
Be bountiful and kill me. You do know
I am a creature hither ill betrayed,

223 **antic** grotesque dance   224 **Ovid's tales** *The Metamorphoses*   225 **Europa** abducted by Jove, who had transformed himself into a bull   226 **Erycine** Venus   232 **Sophy** Shah   233 **Grand Signor** Sultan of Turkey   235 **quick** vigorous   240 **tell** count   242 **be pined** pine with envy

250 By one whose shame I would forget it were.
    If you will deign me neither of these graces,
    Yet feed your wrath, sir, rather than your lust,—
    It is a vice comes nearer manliness—
    And punish that unhappy crime of nature
    Which you miscall my beauty. Flay my face,
    Or poison it with ointments, for seducing
    Your blood to this rebellion. Rub these hands
    With what may cause an eating leprosy,
    E'en to my bones and marrow—anything
260 That may disfavor me, save in my honor.
    And I will kneel to you, pray for you, pay down
    A thousand hourly vows, sir, for your health;
    Report and think you virtuous——
    VOLPONE.   Think me cold,
    Frozen, and impotent, and so report me?
    That I had Nestor's hernia thou wouldst think.
    I do degenerate, and abuse my nation,
    To play with opportunity thus long.
    I should have done the act, and then have parleyed.
    Yield, or I'll force thee.
    CELIA.   O! Just God!
    VOLPONE.   In vain——
270   BONARIO. (*Leaps out from where* MOSCA *had placed him.*) Forbear, foul ravisher! Libidinous swine!
    Free the forced lady or thou diest, impostor.
    But that I am loath to snatch thy punishment
    Out of the hand of justice, thou shouldst yet
    Be made the timely sacrifice of vengeance,
    Before this altar, and this dross, thy idol.—
    Lady, let's quit the place; it is the den
    Of villainy. Fear nought, you have a guard;
    And he ere long shall meet his just reward.
                 [*Exeunt* BONARIO *and* CELIA.]
    VOLPONE. Fall on me, roof, and bury me in ruin!
280 Become my grave, that wert my shelter! O!
    I am unmasked, unspirited, undone,
    Betrayed to beggary, to infamy——

[*Enter* MOSCA, *wounded.*]

    MOSCA. Where shall I run, most wretched shame of men,
To beat out my unlucky brains?

260 **disfavor** disfigure   265 **Nestor's hernia** impotence of old age   266 **I . . . degenerate** I violate my own nature   281 **unspirited** thrown into despondency

VOLPONE.   Here, here.
What! Dost thou bleed?
MOSCA.   O that his well-driv'n sword
Had been so courteous to have cleft me down
Unto the navel, ere I lived to see   .
My life, my hopes, my spirits, my patron, all
Thus desperately engagèd by my error!
    VOLPONE. Woe on thy fortune!
MOSCA.   And my follies, sir.   290
    VOLPONE. Th'ast made me miserable.
MOSCA.   And myself, sir.
Who would have thought he would have hearkened so?
    VOLPONE. What shall we do?
MOSCA.   I know not; if my heart
Could expiate the mischance, I'd pluck it out.
Will you be pleasèd to hang me, or cut my throat?
And I'll requite you, sir. Let's die like Romans,
Since we have lived like Grecians.
                      (*They knock without.*)
    VOLPONE.   Hark! Who's there?
I hear some footing; officers, the *Saffi*,
Come to apprehend us! I do feel the brand
Hissing already at my forehead; now   300
Mine ears are boring.
    MOSCA.   To your couch, sir; you
Make that place good, however. [VOLPONE *lies down as
    before.*] Guilty men
Suspect what they deserve still. Signor Corbaccio!

             [*Enter* CORBACCIO.]

    CORBACCIO. Why, how now, Mosca?
MOSCA.   O, undone, amazed, sir!
Your son,—I know not by what accident—
Acquainted with your purpose to my patron,
Touching your will, and making him your heir,
Entered our house with violence, his sword drawn,
Sought for you, called you wretch, unnatural,
Vowed he would kill you.
    CORBACCIO.   Me?
MOSCA.   Yes, and my patron.   310
    CORBACCIO. This act shall disinherit him indeed!
Here is the will.

289 **engagèd** entrammeled   296 **requite you** reciprocate   **like
Romans** *i.e.*, by our own hands   297 **like Grecians** *i.e.*, riotously
298 **Saffi** Venetian police   301 **boring** being bored through
302 **however** in any case

MOSCA.   'Tis well, sir.
CORBACCIO.   Right and well.
Be you as careful now for me.

[*Enter* VOLTORE, *behind.*]

MOSCA.   My life, sir,
Is not more tendered; I am only yours.
        CORBACCIO. How does he? Will he die shortly, think'st
            thou?
        MOSCA. I fear
He'll outlast May.
        CORBACCIO.   Today?
        MOSCA.   No, last out May, sir.
        CORBACCIO. Couldst thou not gi' him a dram?
        MOSCA.   O, by no means, sir.
        CORBACCIO. Nay, I'll not bid you.
        VOLTORE.   This is a knave, I see.
        MOSCA. [*Aside.*] —How! Signor Voltore! Did he hear
            me?
        VOLTORE. Parasite!
        MOSCA. Who's that?—O sir, most timely welcome—
320   VOLTORE.   Scarce,
To the discovery of your tricks, I fear.
You are his only? And mine also, are you not?
        MOSCA. Who? I, sir!
        VOLTORE.   You, sir. What device is this
About a will?
        MOSCA.   A plot for you, sir.
        VOLTORE.   Come,
Put not your foists upon me; I shall scent 'em.
        MOSCA. Did you not hear it?
        VOLTORE.   Yes, I hear Corbaccio
Hath made your patron there his heir.
        MOSCA.   'Tis true;
By my device, drawn to it by my plot,
With hope——
        VOLTORE.   Your patron should reciprocate?
And you have promised?
330   MOSCA.   For your good I did, sir.
Nay more, I told his son, brought, hid him here,
Where he might hear his father pass the deed;
Being persuaded to it by this thought, sir:
That the unnaturalness, first, of the act,

313 **careful** full of concern   314 **tendered** cared for   325 **foists**
tricks

And then his father's oft disclaiming in him—
Which I did mean t'help on—would sure enrage him
To do some violence upon his parent;
On which the law should take sufficient hold,
And you be stated in a double hope.
Truth be my comfort, and my conscience, 340
My only aim was to dig you a fortune
Out of these two old rotten sepulchres——
    VOLTORE. I cry thee mercy, Mosca.
    MOSCA.   Worth your patience,
And your great merit, sir. And see the change!
    VOLTORE. Why, what success?
    MOSCA.   Most hapless! You must help, sir.
Whilst we expected th' old raven, in comes
Corvino's wife, sent hither by her husband——
    VOLTORE. What, with a present?
    MOSCA.   No, sir, on visitation,—
I'll tell you how anon—and staying long,
The youth he grows impatient, rushes forth, 350
Seizeth the lady, wounds me, makes her swear—
Or he would murder her, that was his vow—
T' affirm my patron to have done her rape;
Which how unlike it is, you see! And hence
With that pretext he's gone, t' accuse his father,
Defame my patron, defeat you——
    VOLTORE.   Where's her husband?
Let him be sent for straight.
    MOSCA.   Sir, I'll go fetch him.
    VOLTORE. Bring him to the *Scrutineo.*
    MOSCA.   Sir, I will.
    VOLTORE. This must be stopped.
    MOSCA.   O, you do nobly, sir.
Alas, 'twas labored all, sir, for your good; 360
Nor was there want of counsel in the plot.
But fortune can, at any time, o'erthrow
The projects of a hundred learnèd clerks, sir.
    CORBACCIO. What's that?
    VOLTORE.   Will't please you, sir, to go along?
           [*Exit* VOLTORE, *followed by* CORBACCIO.]
    MOSCA. Patron, go in and pray for our success.
    VOLPONE. Need makes devotion. Heaven your labor
      bless!   [*Exeunt.*]

335 **disclaiming in** repudiating   339 **stated** installed   345 **success** outcome   358 **Scrutineo** Senate House   363 **clerks** scholars
366 **Need . . . devotion** Desperation fosters piety

Act Four

Scene One

[A *street*]

[*Enter* Sir Politic Wouldbe *and* Peregrine.]

Sir Politic. I told you, sir, it was a plot. You see
What observation is. You mentioned me
For some instructions: I will tell you, sir,
Since we are met here in this height of Venice,
Some few particulars I have set down,
Only for this meridian, fit to be known
Of your crude traveler; and they are these.
I will not touch, sir, at your phrase, or clothes,
For they are old.
    Peregrine.   Sir, I have better.
    Sir Politic.   Pardon,
I meant, as they are themes.
10   Peregrine.   O sir, proceed.
I'll slander you no more of wit, good sir.
    Sir Politic. First, for your garb, it must be grave and
        serious,
Very reserved and locked; not tell a secret
On any terms, not to your father; scarce
A fable, but with caution; make sure choice
Both of your company and discourse; beware
You never speak a truth——
    Peregrine.   How!
    Sir Politic.   Not to strangers,
For those be they you must converse with most;
Others I would not know, sir, but at distance,
20 So as I still might be a saver in 'em;
You shall have tricks else passed upon you hourly.
And then, for your religion, profess none,
But wonder at the diversity of all;
And, for your part, protest, were there no other
But simply the laws o' th' land, you could content you.

1 **it** evidently the scene in which Corvino beats Volpone away
from his window in Act II 12 **garb** outward bearing 19
know acknowledge 20 **So . . . 'em** So that I might preserve
acquaintance with them

Nick Machiavel and Monsieur Bodin both
Were of this mind. Then must you learn the use
And handling of your silver fork at meals,
The metal of your glass,—these are main matters
With your Italian—and to know the hour   30
When you must eat your melons and your figs.
    PEREGRINE. Is that a point of state, too?
    SIR POLITIC.   Here it is
For your Venetian, if he see a man
Preposterous in the least, he has him straight.
He has; he strips him. I'll acquaint you, sir,
I now have lived here 'tis some fourteen months,
Within the first week of my landing here,
All took me for a citizen of Venice.
I knew the forms so well——
    PEREGRINE. [Aside.]   —And nothing else.
    SIR POLITIC. I had read Contarene, took me a house,   40
Dealt with my Jews to furnish it with movables—
Well, if I could but find one man, one man
To mine own heart, whom I durst trust, I would——
    PEREGRINE. What, what, sir?
    SIR POLITIC.   Make him rich; make him a
    fortune.
He should not think again. I would command it.
    PEREGRINE. As how?
    SIR POLITIC.   With certain projects that I have,
Which I may not discover.
    PEREGRINE. [Aside.]   —If I had
But one to wager with, I would lay odds now,
He tells me instantly.
    SIR POLITIC.   One is—and that
I care not greatly who knows—to serve the state   50
Of Venice with red herrings for three years,
And at a certain rate, from Rotterdam,
Where I have correspondence. There's a letter,
Sent me from one o' th' States, and to that purpose.
He cannot write his name, but that's his mark.

---

26 **Machiavel** Machiavelli, Florentine political writer with a reputation for atheism   **Bodin** French political thinker, proponent of religious toleration   28 **fork** not yet in common use in England   29 **metal** material   34 **Preposterous** unconventional   40 **Contarene** Contarini, author of a treatise on the Venetian Republic   47 **discover** disclose   48 **one** someone   54 **one . . . States** member of the States General of Holland

PEREGRINE. He is a chandler?
SIR POLITIC.   No, a cheesemonger.
There are some other, too, with whom I treat
About the same negotiation;
And I will undertake it. For 'tis thus:
60 I'll do't with ease, I've cast it all. Your hoy
Carries but three men in her, and a boy,
And she shall make me three returns a year;
So if there come but one of three, I save;
If two, I can defalc. But this is now,
If my main project fail.
        PEREGRINE.   Then you have others?
        SIR POLITIC. I should be loath to draw the subtle air
Of such a place, without my thousand aims.
I'll not dissemble, sir, where'er I come,
I love to be considerative; and 'tis true
70 I have at my free hours thought upon
Some certain goods unto the state of Venice,
Which I do call my cautions; and, sir, which
I mean, in hope of pension, to propound
To the Great Council, then unto the Forty,
So to the Ten. My means are made already——
        PEREGRINE. By whom?
        SIR POLITIC.   Sir, one that though his place be
        obscure,
Yet he can sway, and they will hear him. He's
A *commendatore*.
        PEREGRINE.   What! A common sergeant?
        SIR POLITIC. Sir, such as they are, put it in their mouths,
80 What they should say, sometimes, as well as greater.
I think I have my notes to show you——
        PEREGRINE.   Good, sir.
        SIR POLITIC. But you shall swear unto me, on your gen-
        try,
Not to anticipate——
        PEREGRINE.   I, sir?
        SIR POLITIC.   Nor reveal
A circumstance——My paper is not with me.
        PEREGRINE. O, but you can remember, sir.
        SIR POLITIC.   My first is
Concerning tinder-boxes. You must know,
No family is here without its box.
Now, sir, it being so portable a thing,

56 **chandler** candle merchant   **cheesemonger** dealer in cheese
60 **cast** calculated   **hoy** small sloop   64 **defalc** cut back ex-
penses   69 **considerative** thoughtful   72 **cautions** precautions

Put case that you or I were ill affected
Unto the state; sir, with it in our pockets,   90
Might not I go into the Arsenal?
Or you? Come out again? And none the wiser?
    PEREGRINE. Except yourself, sir.
    SIR POLITIC.   Go to, then. I therefore
Advertise to the state, how fit it were
That none but such as were known patriots,
Sound lovers of their country, should be suffered
T' enjoy them in their houses; and even those
Sealed at some office, and at such a bigness
As might not lurk in pockets.
    PEREGRINE.   Admirable!
    SIR POLITIC. My next is, how t' inquire, and be resolved 100
By present demonstration, whether a ship,
Newly arrivèd from Syria, or from
Any suspected part of all the Levant,
Be guilty of the plague. And, where they use
To lie out forty, fifty days, sometimes,
About the *Lazaretto,* for their trial;
I'll save that charge and loss unto the merchant,
And in an hour clear the doubt.
    PEREGRINE.   Indeed, sir!
    SIR POLITIC. Or——I will lose my labor.
    PEREGRINE.   My faith, that's much.
    SIR POLITIC. Nay, sir, conceive me. 'Twill cost me, in 110
    onions,
Some thirty livres——
    PEREGRINE.   Which is one pound sterling.
    SIR POLITIC. Beside my waterworks. For this I do, sir:
First, I bring in your ship 'twixt two brick walls—
But those the state shall venture. On the one
I strain me a fair tarpaulin, and in that
I stick my onions, cut in halves; the other
Is full of loopholes, out at which I thrust
The noses of my bellows; and those bellows
I keep, with waterworks, in perpetual motion,
Which is the easiest matter of a hundred.   120
Now, sir, your onion, which doth naturally
Attract th' infection, and your bellows blowing
The air upon him, will show instantly,
By his changed color, if there be contagion;
Or else remain as fair as at the first.

101 **present** immediate 103 **Levant** the East 106 **Lazaretto**
quarantine island 111 **livres** French money 115 **strain** stretch
123 **him** it

Now 'tis known, 'tis nothing.
    PEREGRINE.   You are right, sir.
    SIR POLITIC. I would I had my note.
    PEREGRINE.   Faith, so would I.—
But you ha' done well for once, sir.
    SIR POLITIC.   Were I false,
Or would be made so, I could show you reasons
130 How I could sell this state now to the Turk,
Spite of their galleys, or their——
    PEREGRINE.   Pray you, Sir Poll.
    SIR POLITIC. I have 'em not about me.
    PEREGRINE.   That I feared.
They 're there, sir?
    SIR POLITIC.   No, this is my diary,
Wherein I note my actions of the day.
    PEREGRINE. Pray you let's see, sir. What is here?—*"No-
        tandum,*
A rat had gnawn my spur-leathers; notwithstanding,
I put on new, and did go forth; but first
I threw three beans over the threshold. Item,
I went and bought two toothpicks, whereof one
140 I burst immediately, in a discourse
With a Dutch merchant, 'bout *ragion del stato.*
From him I went and paid a *moccenigo*
For piecing my silk stocking; by the way
I cheapened sprats; and at St. Mark's I urined."
Faith these are politic notes!
    SIR POLITIC.   Sir, I do slip
No action of my life, thus, but I quote it.
    PEREGRINE. Believe me, it is wise!
    SIR POLITIC.   Nay, sir, read forth.

      [*Enter* LADY WOULDBE, NANO, *and two* WOMEN.]

    LADY WOULDBE. Where should this loose knight be,
    trow? Sure, he's housed.
    NANO. Why, then he's fast.
    LADY WOULDBE.   Ay, he plays both with me!
150 I pray you stay.—This heat will do more harm
To my complexion than his heart is worth.
I do not care to hinder, but to take him.
How it comes off!
    1ST WOMAN. My master's yonder.

141 **ragion del stato** affairs of state   143 **piecing** mending   144
cheapened bargained for   145 **slip** pass over   149 **plays both**
i.e., plays fast and loose   153 **it** her "complexion"

LADY WOULDBE.   Where?
2ND WOMAN. With a young gentleman.
LADY WOULDBE.   That same's the party,
In man's apparel!—Pray you, sir, jog my knight.
I will be tender to his reputation,
However he demerit.
    SIR POLITIC.   —My lady!
    PEREGRINE.   Where?
    SIR POLITIC. 'Tis she indeed, sir, you shall know her.
    She is,
Were she not mine, a lady of that merit,
For fashion and behavior; and for beauty   160
I durst compare——
    PEREGRINE.   It seems you are not jealous,
That dare commend her.
    SIR POLITIC.   Nay, and for discourse——
    PEREGRINE. Being your wife, she cannot miss that.
    SIR POLITIC.   Madam,
Here is a gentleman, pray you, use him fairly;
He seems a youth, but he is——
    LADY WOULDBE.   None.
    SIR POLITIC.   Yes, one
Has put his face as soon into the world——
    LADY WOULDBE. You mean, as early? But today?
    SIR POLITIC.   How's this?
    LADY WOULDBE. Why, in this habit, sir, you apprehend
    me.
Well, Master Wouldbe, this doth not become you.
I had thought the odor, sir, of your good name   170
Had been more precious to you; that you would not
Have done this dire massàcre on your honor;
One of your gravity, and rank besides!
But knights, I see, care little for the oath
They make to ladies, chiefly their own ladies.
    SIR POLITIC. Now, by my spurs, the symbol of my
    knighthood——
    PEREGRINE. [*Aside.*] —Lord, how his brain is humbled
    for an oath!
    SIR POLITIC. I reach you not.
    LADY WOULDBE.   Right, sir, your policy
May bear it through thus. [*To* PEREGRINE.] —Sir, a word
    with you.
I would be loath to còntest publicly   180

157 **However . . . demerit** however much he is at fault   178
I . . . not I don't understand you   178 **policy** cunning

With any gentlewoman, or to seem
Froward, or violent, as the courtier says—
It comes too near rusticity in a lady,
Which I would shun by all means. And, however
I may deserve from Master Wouldbe, yet
T' have one fair gentlewoman thus be made
Th' unkind instrument to wrong another,
And one she knows not, ay, and to persèver;
In my poor judgment, is not warranted
190 From being a solecism in our sex,
If not in manners.
    PEREGRINE.   How is this!
    SIR POLITIC.   Sweet madam,
Come nearer to your aim.
    LADY WOULDBE.   Marry, and will, sir.
Since you provoke me with your impudence,
And laughter of your light land-siren here,
Your Sporus, your hermaphrodite——
    PEREGRINE.   What's here?
Poetic fury and historic storms!
    SIR POLITIC. The gentleman, believe it, is of worth,
And of our nation.
    LADY WOULDBE. Ay, your Whitefriars nation!
Come, I blush for you, Master Wouldbe, I;
200 And am ashamed you should ha' no more forehead
Than thus to be the patron, or St. George,
To a lewd harlot, a base fricatrice,
A female devil in a male outside.
    SIR POLITIC.   Nay,
And you be such a one, I must bid adieu
To your delights. The case appears too liquid.   [Exit.]
    LADY WOULDBE. Ay, you may carry't clear, with your
       state-face!
But for your carnival concupiscence,

---

182 **the courtier** title of a treatise on conduct for the nobility
by Castiglione   194 **light** loose   195 **Sporus** favorite of the
Emperor Nero, who had him emasculated, dressed him as a
woman, and publicly married him   198 **Whitefriars nation**
community of petty criminals inhabiting the Whitefriars quarter
of London   200 **forehead** shame   202 **fricatrice** prostitute
205 **liquid** clear   206 **state-face** official countenance   207
your . . . concupiscence roughly "this wench, as licentious as
a carnival, on whom you have fixed your lust"

Who here is fled for liberty of conscience,
From furious persecution of the Marshal,
Her will I disc'ple.
    PEREGRINE   This is fine, i' faith!   210
And do you use this often? Is this part
Of your wit's exercise, 'gainst you have occasion?
Madam——
    LADY WOULDBE. Go to, sir.
    PEREGRINE.   Do you hear me, lady?
Why, if your knight have set you to beg shirts,
Or to invite me home, you might have done it
A nearer way by far.
    LADY WOULDBE. This cannot work you
Out of my snare.
    PEREGRINE.   Why, am I in it, then?
Indeed your husband told me you were fair,
And so you are; only your nose inclines—
That side that's next the sun—to the queen-apple.   220
    LADY WOULDBE. This cannot be endured by any
      patience.

               [*Enter* MOSCA.]

    MOSCA. What's the matter, madam?
    LADY WOULDBE.   If the Senate
Right not my quest in this, I will protest 'em
To all the world no aristocracy.
    MOSCA. What is the injury, lady?
    LADY WOULDBE.   Why, the callet
You told me of, here I have ta'en disguised.
    MOSCA. Who? This! What means your ladyship? The
      creature
I mentioned to you is apprehended now
Before the Senate. You shall see her——
    LADY WOULDBE.   Where?
    MOSCA. I'll bring you to her. This young gentleman,   230
I saw him land this morning at the port.
    LADY WOULDBE. Is't possible? How has my judgment
      wandered!
Sir, I must, blushing, say to you I have erred,

---

208 **fled . . . Marshal** like the Puritans. Lady Wouldbe means
that Peregrine is an English prostitute in disguise who has fled
to Venice in order to practice her trade more freely.   210
disc'ple discipline   212 **'gainst . . . occasion** in preparation for
when you need it   216 **a . . . way** more directly   219 **nose
. . . queen-apple** *i.e.,* your nose is red   225 **callet** strumpet

And plead your pardon.

PEREGRINE.   What, more changes yet?

LADY WOULDBE. I hope y' ha' not the malice to remember
A gentlewoman's passion. If you stay
In Venice here, please you to use me, sir——

MOSCA. Will you go, madam?

LADY WOULDBE.   Pray you, sir, use me. In faith,
The more you see me, the more I shall conceive
You have forgot our quarrel.

                                        [*Exeunt* LADY WOULDBE, MOSCA, NANO,
                                                      and WOMEN.]

240   PEREGRINE.   This is rare!
Sir Politic Wouldbe? No, Sir Politic Bawd,
To bring me thus acquainted with his wife!
Well, wise Sir Poll, since you have practiced thus
Upon my freshmanship, I'll try your salt-head,
What proof it is against a counter-plot.   [*Exit.*]

SCENE TWO

[*The Scrutineo*]

[*Enter* VOLTORE, CORBACCIO, CORVINO, *and* MOSCA.]

VOLTORE. Well, now you know the carriage of the
          business,
Your constancy is all that is required
Unto the safety of it.

MOSCA.   Is the lie
Safely conveyed amongst us? Is that sure?
Knows every man his burden?

CORVINO.   Yes.

MOSCA.   Then shrink not.

CORVINO. [*Aside to* MOSCA.] —But knows the advocate
          the truth?

MOSCA.   O sir,
By no means. I devised a formal tale
That salved your reputation. But be valiant, sir.

CORVINO. I fear no one but him, that this his pleading
10 Should make him stand for a co-heir——

MOSCA.   Co-halter!
Hang him, we will but use his tongue, his noise,
As we do Croaker's here.

CORVINO.   Ay, what shall he do?

MOSCA. When we have done, you mean?

241 **Bawd** pander   243 **practiced** plotted   244 **salt-head** "salt-
hood," "veteranship" as opposed to "freshmanship"   7 **formal**
convincingly circumstantial   12 **Croaker** Corbaccio

CORVINO.   Yes.
MOSCA.   Why, we'll think:
Sell him for mummia; he's half dust already. (*To* VOL-
    TORE.)
Do not you smile to see this buffalo,
How he doth sport it with his head?—I should,
If all were well and past. (*To* CORBACCIO.) Sir, only you
Are he that shall enjoy the crop of all,
And these not know for whom they toil.
    CORBACCIO.   Ay, peace.
    MOSCA. (*To* CORVINO.) But you shall eat it. [*Aside.*]
    —Much!— (*To* VOLTORE.) Worshipful sir,   20
Mercury sit upon your thund'ring tongue,
Or the French Hercules, and make your language
As conquering as his club, to beat along,
As with a tempest, flat, our adversaries;
But much more yours, sir.
    VOLTORE.   Here they come, ha' done.
    MOSCA. I have another witness, if you need, sir,
I can produce.
    VOLTORE.   Who is it?
    MOSCA.   Sir, I have her.

    [*Enter four* AVOCATORI, BONARIO, CELIA, NOTARIO,
                COMMENDATORI, *&c.*]

    1ST AVOCATORE. The like of this the Senate never heard
        of.
    2ND AVOCATORE. 'Twill come most strange to them,
        when we report it.
    4TH AVOCATORE. The gentlewoman has been ever held 30
Of unreprovèd name.
    3RD AVOCATORE. So the young man.
    4TH AVOCATORE. The more unnatural part that of his
        father.
    2ND AVOCATORE. More of the husband.
    1ST AVOCATORE.   I not know to give
His act a name, it is so monstrous!
    4TH AVOCATORE. But the impostor, he is a thing created
T' exceed example!
    1ST AVOCATORE. And all after-times!
    2ND AVOCATORE. I never heard a true voluptuary
Described, but him.

14 **mummia** extract from embalmed bodies, prized as a medicine
15 **buffalo** Corvino, because of his horns   21 **Mercury** god of
eloquence   22 **French Hercules** symbol of eloquence   33 **I
. . . know** I do not know how   34 **monstrous** here pronounced
"monsterous"

3RD AVOCATORE. Appear yet those were cited?

NOTARIO. All but the old magnifico, Volpone.

1ST AVOCATORE. Why is not he here?

40 MOSCA.   Please your fatherhoods,
Here is his advocate. Himself's so weak,
So feeble——

4TH AVOCATORE. What are you?

BONARIO.   His parasite,
His knave, his pander! I beseech the court
He may be forced to come, that your grave eyes
May bear strong witness of his strange impostures.

VOLTORE. Upon my faith and credit with your virtues,
He is not able to endure the air.

2ND AVOCATORE. Bring him, however.

3RD AVOCATORE.   We will see him.

4TH AVOCATORE. Fetch him.   [*Exeunt* OFFICERS.]

VOLTORE. Your fatherhoods' fit pleasures be obeyed,
50 But sure the sight will rather move your pities
Than indignation. May it please the court,
In the meantime, he may be heard in me:
I know this place most void of prejudice,
And therefore crave it, since we have no reason
To fear our truth should hurt our cause.

3RD AVOCATORE.   Speak free.

VOLTORE. Then know, most honored fathers, I must now
Discover to your strangely abusèd ears
The most prodigious and most frontless piece
Of solid impudence and treachery
60 That ever vicious nature yet brought forth
To shame the state of Venice. This lewd woman,
That wants no artificial looks or tears
To help the visor she has now put on,
Hath long been known a close adulteress
To that lascivious youth there; not suspected,
I say, but known, and taken in the act
With him; and by this man, the easy husband,
Pardoned; whose timeless bounty makes him now
Stand here, the most unhappy, innocent person
70 That ever man's own goodness made accused.
For these, not knowing how to owe a gift
Of that dear grace, but with their shame; being placed
So above all powers of their gratitude,
Began to hate the benefit; and in place
Of thanks, devise t' extirp the memory

39 **magnifico** Venetian nobleman 57 **abusèd** deluded 58
frontless shameless 64 **close** secret 68 **timeless** ill-timed
72 **dear grace** preciousness 75 **extirp** root out

Of such an act. Wherein, I pray your fatherhoods
To observe the malice, yea, the rage of creatures
Discovered in their evils; and what heart
Such take, even from their crimes. But that anon
Will more appear. This gentleman, the father, 80
Hearing of this foul fact, with many others,
Which daily struck at his too tender ears,
And grieved in nothing more than that he could not
Preserve himself a parent,—his son's ills
Growing to that strange flood—at last decreed
To disinherit him.
   1st Avocatore. These be strange turns!
   2nd Avocatore. The young man's fame was ever fair
      and honest.
   Voltore. So much more full of danger is his vice,
That can beguile so, under shade of virtue.
But, as I said, my honored sires, his father 90
Having this settled purpose,—by what means
To him betrayed, we know not—and this day
Appointed for the deed; that parricide,
I cannot style him better, by confederacy
Preparing this his paramour to be there,
Entered Volpone's house,—who was the man,
Your fatherhoods must understand, designed
For the inheritance—there sought his father.
But with what purpose sought he him, my lords?
I tremble to pronounce it, that a son 100
Unto a father, and to such a father,
Should have so foul, felonious intent:
It was to murder him! When, being prevented
By his more happy absence, what then did he?
Not check his wicked thoughts; no, now new deeds,—
Mischief doth never end where it begins—
An act of horror, fathers! He dragged forth
The agèd gentleman that had there lain bed-rid
Three years and more, out off his innocent couch,
Naked, upon the floor, there left him; wounded 110
His servant in the face; and with this strumpet,
The stale to his forged practice, who was glad
To be so active,—I shall here desire
Your fatherhoods to note but my collections,
As most remarkable—thought at once to stop
His father's ends, discredit his free choice
In the old gentleman, redeem themselves
By laying infamy upon this man,
To whom, with blushing, they should owe their lives.

81 **fact** crime   112 **stale** decoy   114 **collections** conclusions

1ST AVOCATORE. What proofs have you of this?

120 BONARIO.   Most honored fathers,
I humbly crave there be no credit given
To this man's mercenary tongue.

2ND AVOCATORE.   Forbear.

BONARIO. His soul moves in his fee.

3RD AVOCATORE.   O, sir!

BONARIO.   This fellow,
For six sols more would plead against his Maker.

1ST AVOCATORE. You do forget yourself.

VOLTORE.   Nay, nay, grave fathers,
Let him have scope. Can any man imagine
That he will spare 's accuser, that would not
Have spared his parent?

1ST AVOCATORE.   Well, produce your proofs.

CELIA. —I would I could forget I were a creature!

VOLTORE. Signor Corbaccio!

4TH AVOCATORE.   What is he?

130 VOLTORE.   The father.

2ND AVOCATORE. Has he had an oath?

NOTARIO.   Yes.

CORBACCIO.   What must I do now?

NOTARIO. Your testimony's craved.

CORBACCIO.   Speak to the knave?
I'll ha' my mouth first stopped with earth. My heart
Abhors his knowledge. I disclaim in him.

1ST AVOCATORE. But for what cause?

CORBACCIO.   The mere portent of nature.
He is an utter stranger to my loins.

BONARIO. Have they made you to this?

CORBACCIO.   I will not hear thee,
Monster of men, swine, goat, wolf, parricide!
Speak not, thou viper.

BONARIO.   Sir, I will sit down,
140 And rather wish my innocence should suffer,
Than I resist the authority of a father.

VOLTORE. Signor Corvino!

2ND AVOCATORE.   This is strange.

1ST AVOCATORE.   Who's this?

NOTARIO. The husband.

4TH AVOCATORE.   Is he sworn?

NOTARIO.   He is.

3RD AVOCATORE.   Speak, then.

124 **sols** pence   135 **mere portent** absolute monster   137 **made**
i.e., suborned

CORVINO. This woman, please your fatherhoods, is a
    whore
Of most hot exercise, more than a partridge,
Upon recòrd——
    1ST AVOCATORE. No more.
    CORVINO.   Neighs like a jennet.
    NOTARIO. Preserve the honor of the court.
    CORVINO.   I shall,
And modesty of your most reverend ears.
And yet I hope that I may say these eyes
Have seen her glued unto that piece of cedar,   150
That fine, well-timbered gallant; and that here
The letters may be read, thorough the horn,
That make the story perfect.
    MOSCA. [*Aside*.]   —Excellent, sir!
    CORVINO. —There is no shame in this now, is there?
    MOSCA.   None.
    CORVINO. Or if I said, I hoped that she were onward
To her damnation, if there be a hell
Greater than whore and woman; a good Catholic
May make the doubt.
    3RD AVOCATORE.   His grief hath made him frantic.
    1ST AVOCATORE. Remove him hence.
                          (CELIA *swoons*.)
    2ND AVOCATORE.   Look to the woman.
    CORVINO.   Rare!
Prettily feigned again!
    4TH AVOCATORE.   Stand from about her.   160
    1ST AVOCATORE. Give her the air.
    3RD AVOCATORE. [*To* MOSCA.]   What can you say?
    MOSCA.   My wound,
May 't please your wisdoms, speaks for me, received
In aid of my good patron, when he missed
His sought-for father, when that well-taught dame
Had her cue given her to cry out a rape.
    BONARIO. O most laid impudence! Fathers—
    3RD AVOCATORE.   Sir, be silent;
You had your hearing free, so must they theirs.
    2ND AVOCATORE. I do begin to doubt th' imposture here.
    4TH AVOCATORE. This woman has too many moods.
    VOLTORE.   Grave fathers,

145 **partridge** proverbially lecherous   146 **Neighs . . . jennet**
i.e., in heat   151 **here . . . horn** Corvino makes the letter V,
the sign of horns, the badge of the cuckold, on his forehead
153 **perfect** complete   166 **laid** well-planned   168 **doubt** suspect

170 She is a creature of a most professed
And prostituted lewdness.
    CORVINO.   Most impetuous,
Unsatisfied, grave fathers!
    VOLTORE.   May her feignings
Not take your wisdoms; but this day she baited
A stranger, a grave knight, with her loose eyes
And more lascivious kisses. This man saw 'em
Together on the water in a gondola.
    MOSCA. Here is the lady herself, that saw 'em too,
Without; who then had in the open streets
Pursued them, but for saving her knight's honor.
    1ST AVOCATORE. Produce that lady.
    2ND AVOCATORE.   Let her come. [*Exit* MOSCA.]
180   4TH AVOCATORE.   These things,
They strike with wonder!
    3RD AVOCATORE.   I am turned a stone!

[*Re-enter* MOSCA *with* LADY WOULDBE.]

    MOSCA. Be resolute, madam.
    LADY WOULDBE.   Ay, this same is she.—
Out, thou chameleon harlot! Now thine eyes
Vie tears with the hyena. Dar'st thou look
Upon my wrongèd face?—I cry your pardons.
I fear I have forgettingly transgressed
Against the dignity of the court——
    2ND AVOCATORE.   No, madam,
    LADY WOULDBE. And been exorbitant——
    4TH AVOCATORE.   You have not, lady,
These proofs are strong.
    LADY WOULDBE.   Surely, I had no purpose
190 To scandalize your honors, or my sex's.
    3RD AVOCATORE. We do believe it.
    LADY WOULDBE.   Surely you may believe it.
    2ND AVOCATORE. Madam, we do.
    LADY WOULDBE.   Indeed you may, my breeding
Is not so coarse——
    4TH AVOCATORE. We know it.
    LADY WOULDBE.   To offend
With pertinacy——
    3RD AVOCATORE. Lady——
    LADY WOULDBE.   Such a presence!
No surely.
    1ST AVOCATORE. We well think it.

188 **exorbitant** out of order   194 **pertinacy** pertinacity

LADY WOULDBE. You may think it.

1ST AVOCATORE. Let her o'ercome.—What witnesses have you,

To make good your report?

BONARIO. Our consciences.

CELIA. And heaven, that never fails the innocent.

4TH AVOCATORE. These are no testimonies.

BONARIO. Not in your courts,

Where multitude and clamor overcomes. 200

1ST AVOCATORE. Nay, then you do wax insolent.

(VOLPONE *is brought in, as impotent.*)

VOLTORE. Here, here

The testimony comes that will convince,
And put to utter dumbness their bold tongues!
See here, grave fathers, here's the ravisher,
The rider on men's wives, the great impostor,
The grand voluptuary! Do you not think
These limbs should affect venery? Or these eyes
Covet a concubine? Pray you mark these hands;
Are they not fit to stroke a lady's breasts?
Perhaps he doth dissemble!

BONARIO. So he does. 210

VOLTORE. Would you ha' him tortured?

BONARIO. I would have him proved.

VOLTORE. Best try him then with goads, or burning irons;
Put him to the strappado. I have heard
The rack hath cured the gout—faith, give it him,
And help him of a malady; be courteous.
I'll undertake, before these honored fathers,
He shall have yet as many left diseases
As she has known adulterers, or thou strumpets.
O my most equal hearers, if these deeds,
Acts of this bold and most exorbitant strain, 220
May pass with sufferance, what one citizen
But owes the forfeit of his life, yea, fame,
To him that dares traduce him? Which of you
Are safe, my honored fathers? I would ask,
With leave of your grave fatherhoods, if their plot
Have any face or color like to truth?
Or if, unto the dullest nostril here,
It smell not rank and most abhorrèd slander?
I crave your care of this good gentleman,

213 **strappado** torture similar to the rack 219 **equal** just

230 Whose life is much endangered by their fable;
And as for them, I will conclude with this:
That vicious persons, when they are hot, and fleshed
In impious acts, their constancy abounds.
Damned deeds are done with greatest confidence.
    1st Avocatore. Take 'em to custody, and sever them.
    2nd Avocatore. 'Tis pity two such prodigies should live.
    1st Avocatore. Let the old gentleman be returned with
      care.   [*Exeunt* Officers *with* Volpone.]
I'm sorry our credulity wronged him.
    4th Avocatore. These are two creatures!
    3rd Avocatore.   I have an earthquake in me!
240   2nd Avocatore. Their shame, even in their cradles, fled
      their faces.
    4th Avocatore. [*To* Voltore.] You've done a worthy
      service to the state, sir,
In their discovery.
    1st Avocatore. You shall hear ere night
What punishment the court decrees upon 'em.
      [*Exeunt* Avocatori, Notario, *and* Commendatori
                          with Bonario *and* Celia.]
    Voltore. We thank your fatherhoods.—How like you it?
    Mosca.   Rare.
I'd ha' your tongue, sir, tipped with gold for this;
I'd ha' you be the heir to the whole city;
The earth I'd have want men, ere you want living.
They're bound to erect your statue in St. Mark's.—
Signor Corvino, I would have you go
And show yourself, that you have conquered.
250   Corvino.   Yes.
    Mosca. It was much better that you should profess
Yourself a cuckold thus, than that the other
Should have been proved.
    Corvino.   Nay, I considered that.
Now it is her fault.
    Mosca.   Then it had been yours.
    Corvino. True. I do doubt this advocate still.
    Mosca.   I' faith,
You need not; I dare ease you of that care.
    Corvino. I trust thee, Mosca.   [*Exit*.]
    Mosca.   As your own soul, sir.
    Corbaccio.   Mosca!
    Mosca. Now for your business, sir.
    Corbaccio.   How! Ha' you business?

232 **fleshed** hardened   247 **want** lack

MOSCA. Yes, yours, sir.
CORBACCIO.   O, none else?
MOSCA.   None else, not I.
CORBACCIO. Be careful, then.
MOSCA.   Rest you with both your eyes, sir. 260
CORBACCIO. Dispatch it.
MOSCA.   Instantly.
CORBACCIO.   And look that all
Whatever be put in, jewels, plate, moneys,
Household stuff, bedding, curtains.
MOSCA.   Curtain-rings, sir;
Only the advocate's fee must be deducted.
   CORBACCIO. I'll pay him now; you'll be too prodigal.
   MOSCA. Sir, I must tender it.
CORBACCIO.   Two chequins is well?
MOSCA. No, six, sir.
CORBACCIO.   'Tis too much.
MOSCA.   He talked a great while,
You must consider that, sir.
CORBACCIO.   Well, there's three——
MOSCA. I'll give it him.
CORBACCIO.   Do so, and there's for thee.
                                                [Exit.]
   MOSCA. Bountiful bones! What horrid strange offense   270
Did he commit 'gainst nature, in his youth,
Worthy this age? [To VOLTORE.] —You see, sir, how I work
Unto your ends; take you no notice.
   VOLTORE.   No,
I'll leave you.   [Exit.]
   MOSCA.   All is yours, the devil and all,
Good advocate!—Madam, I'll bring you home.
   LADY WOULDBE. No, I'll go see your patron.
   MOSCA.   That you shall not.
I'll tell you why: my purpose is to urge
My patron to reform his will, and for
The zeal you've shown today, whereas before
You were but third or fourth, you shall be now   280
Put in the first; which would appear as begged
If you were present. Therefore——
   LADY WOULDBE.   You shall sway me.
                                                [Exeunt.]

Act Five

SCENE ONE

[*Volpone's house*]

[*Enter* VOLPONE.]

VOLPONE. Well, I am here, and all this brunt is past.
I ne'er was in dislike with my disguise
Till this fled moment. Here 'twas good, in private;
But in your public—*Cavè*, whilst I breathe.
'Fore God, my left leg 'gan to have the cramp,
And I apprehended straight some power had struck me
With a dead palsy. Well, I must be merry,
And shake it off. A many of these fears
Would put me into some villainous disease,
10 Should they come thick upon me. I'll prevent 'em.
Give me a bowl of lusty wine, to fright
This humor from my heart. (*Drinks.*) Hum, hum, hum!
'Tis almost gone already; I shall conquer.
Any device, now, of rare, ingenious knavery,
That would possess me with a violent laughter,
Would make me up again. (*Drinks again.*) So, so, so, so!
This heat is life; 'tis blood by this time!—Mosca!

[*Enter* MOSCA.]

MOSCA. How now, sir! Does the day look clear again?
Are we recovered, and wrought out of error,
20 Into our way, to see our path before us?
Is our trade free once more?
    VOLPONE.   Exquisite Mosca!
    MOSCA. Was it not carried learnedly?
    VOLPONE.   And stoutly.
Good wits are greatest in extremities.
    MOSCA. It were a folly beyond thought, to trust
Any grand act unto a cowardly spirit.
You are not taken with it enough, methinks.
    VOLPONE. O, more than if I had enjoyed the wench.
The pleasure of all womankind's not like it.
    MOSCA. Why, now you speak, sir! We must here be
        fixed;
30 Here we must rest. This is our masterpiece;

4 **Cavè** Beware

We cannot think to go beyond this.
VOLPONE.   True,
Th'ast played thy prize, my precious Mosca.
MOSCA.   Nay, sir,
To gull the court——
VOLPONE.   And quite divert the torrent
Upon the innocent.
MOSCA.   Yes, and to make
So rare a music out of discords——
VOLPONE.   Right.
That yet to me's the strangest; how th'ast borne it!
That these, being so divided 'mongst themselves,
Should not scent somewhat, or in me or thee,
Or doubt their own side.
MOSCA.   True, they will not see't.
Too much light blinds 'em, I think. Each of 'em   **40**
Is so possessed and stuffed with his own hopes
That anything unto the contrary,
Never so true, or never so apparent,
Never so palpable, they will resist it——
VOLPONE. Like a temptation of the devil.
MOSCA.   Right, sir.
Merchants may talk of trade, and your great signors
Of land that yields well; but if Italy
Have any glebe more fruitful than these fellows,
I am deceived. Did not your advocate rare?
VOLPONE. O—"My most honored fathers, my grave fa- **50**
   thers,
Under correction of your fatherhoods,
What face of truth is here? If these strange deeds
May pass, most honored fathers"—I had much ado
To forbear laughing.
MOSCA.   'T seemed to me you sweat, sir.
VOLPONE. In troth, I did a little.
MOSCA.   But confess, sir
Were you not daunted?
VOLPONE.   In good faith, I was
A little in a mist, but not dejected;
Never, but still myself.
MOSCA.   I think it, sir.
Now, so truth help me, I must needs say this, sir,
And out of conscience for your advocate: **60**
He 's taken pains, in faith, sir, and deserved,
In my poor judgment, I speak it under favor,

48 **glebe** soil   53 **pass** be allowed

Not to contrary you, sir, very richly—
Well—to be cozened.
    VOLPONE.   Troth, and I think so too,
By that I heard him in the latter end.
    MOSCA. O, but before, sir, had you heard him first
Draw it to certain heads, then aggravate,
Then use his vehement figures—I looked still
When he would shift a shirt; and doing this
Out of pure love, no hope of gain——
70   VOLPONE.   'Tis right.
I cannot answer him, Mosca, as I would,
Not yet; but for thy sake, at thy entreaty,
I will begin ev'n now—to vex 'em all,
This very instant.
    MOSCA.   Good, sir.
    VOLPONE.   Call the dwarf
And eunuch forth.
    MOSCA.   Castrone! Nano!

[Enter CASTRONE and NANO.]

    NANO.   Here.
    VOLPONE. Shall we have a jig now?
    MOSCA.   What you please, sir.
    VOLPONE.   Go,
Straight give out about the streets, you two,
That I am dead; do it with constancy,
Sadly, do you hear? Impute it to the grief
Of this late slander.   [Exeunt CASTRONE and NANO.]
    MOSCA.   What do you mean, sir?
80   VOLPONE.   O,
I shall have instantly my vulture, crow,
Raven, come flying hither, on the news,
To peck for carrion, my she-wolf and all,
Greedy and full of expectation——
    MOSCA. And then to have it ravished from their mouths?
    VOLPONE. 'Tis true. I will ha' thee put on a gown,
And take upon thee as thou wert mine heir;
Show 'em a will. Open that chest, and reach
Forth one of those that has the blanks. I'll straight
Put in thy name.
    MOSCA.   It will be rare, sir.

64 **cozened** cheated   67 **Draw . . . heads** collect his argument
into topics **aggravate** emphasize 68 **figures** *i.e.,* of rhetoric
69 **shift a shirt** *i.e.,* through the violence of his gestures 71
answer repay 79 **sadly** seriously

VOLPONE.   Ay,   90
When they e'en gape, and find themselves deluded——
MOSCA. Yes.
VOLPONE.   And thou use them scurvily! Dispatch,
Get on thy gown.
MOSCA.   But what, sir, if they ask
After the body?
VOLPONE.   Say it was corrupted.
MOSCA. I'll say it stunk, sir; and was fain t' have it
Coffined up instantly, and sent away.
VOLPONE. Anything, what thou wilt. Hold, here's my
    will.
Get thee a cap, a count-book, pen and ink,
Papers afore thee; sit as thou wert taking
An inventory of parcels. I'll get up   100
Behind the curtain, on a stool, and hearken;
Sometime peep over, see how they do look,
With what degrees their blood doth leave their faces.
O, 'twill afford me a rare meal of laughter!
MOSCA. Your advocate will turn stark dull upon it.
VOLPONE. It will take off his oratory's edge.
MOSCA. But your *clarissimo,* old round-back, he
Will crump you like a hog-louse with the touch.
VOLPONE. And what Corvino?
MOSCA.   O sir, look for him
Tomorrow morning, with a rope and dagger,   110
To visit all the streets; he must run mad.
My lady too, that came into the court
To bear false witness for your worship——
VOLPONE.   Yes,
And kissed me 'fore the fathers, when my face
Flowed all with oils——
MOSCA.   And sweat, sir. Why, your gold
Is such another med'cine, it dries up
All those offensive savors! It transforms
The most deformèd, and restores 'em lovely
As 'twere the strange poetical girdle. Jove
Could not invent t' himself a shroud more subtle   120
To pass Acrisius' guards. It is the thing
Makes all the world her grace, her youth, her beauty.

---

98 **count-book** account book   107 **clarissimo** Venetian grandee
108 **crump you** curl up   119 **poetical girdle** worn by Venus,
with love and beauty woven into it   **Jove . . . guards** Jove
penetrated the locked chamber of Danae, daughter of Acrisius,
by transforming himself into a shower of gold

VOLPONE. I think she loves me.
MOSCA.   Who? The lady, sir?
She's jealous of you.
VOLPONE.   Dost thou say so? [*Knocking without.*]
MOSCA.   Hark,
There's some already.
VOLPONE.   Look.
MOSCA.   It is the vulture;
He has the quickest scent.
VOLPONE.   I'll to my place,
Thou to thy posture.
MOSCA.   I am set.
VOLPONE.   But, Mosca,
Play the artificer, now, torture 'em rarely.

[*Enter* VOLTORE.]

VOLTORE. How now, my Mosca?
MOSCA. [*Writing.*]   "Turkey carpets, nine——"
130 VOLTORE. Taking an inventory? That is well.
MOSCA. "Two suits of bedding, tissue——"
VOLTORE.   Where's the will?
Let me read that the while.

[*Enter* SERVITORI *with* CORBACCIO *in a chair.*]

CORBACCIO.   So, set me down,
And get you home.   [*Exeunt* SERVITORI.]
VOLTORE.   Is he come now, to trouble us?
MOSCA. "Of cloth of gold, two more——"
CORBACCIO.   Is it done, Mosca?
MOSCA. "Of several velvets, eight——"
VOLTORE.   I like his care.
CORBACCIO. Dost thou not hear?

[*Enter* CORVINO.]

CORVINO.   Ha! Is the hour come, Mosca?
VOLPONE. (*Peeps from behind a traverse.*) Ay, now
    they muster.
CORVINO.   What does the advocate here,
Or this Corbaccio?
CORBACCIO.   What do these here?

[*Enter* LADY WOULDBE.]

LADY WOULDBE.   Mosca!
Is his thread spun?
128 **artificer** trickster   131 **suits** sets   **tissue** cloth woven with
gold   137 s.d. **traverse** low curtain or screen

MOSCA. "Eight chests of linen——"
VOLPONE.   —O,
My fine Dame Wouldbe, too!
CORVINO.   Mosca, the will,   140
That I may show it these, and rid 'em hence.
MOSCA. "Six chests of diaper, four of damask—" There.
  [*Gives them the will carelessly.*]
CORBACCIO. Is that the will?
MOSCA.   "Down-beds, and bolsters——"
VOLPONE.   —Rare!
Be busy still. Now they begin to flutter;
They never think of me. Look, see, see, see!
How their swift eyes run over the long deed,
Unto the name, and to the legacies,
What is bequeathed them there——
MOSCA.   "Ten suits of hangings——"
VOLPONE. —Ay, i' their garters, Mosca. Now their hopes
Are at the gasp.
VOLTORE.   Mosca the heir!
CORBACCIO.   What's that?   150
VOLPONE. —My advocate is dumb; look to my merchant,
He has heard of some strange storm, a ship is lost,
He faints; my lady will swoon. Old glazen-eyes
He hath not reached his despair yet.
CORBACCIO.   All these
Are out of hope; I'm sure the man.
CORVINO.   But, Mosca——
MOSCA. "Two cabinets——"
CORVINO.   Is this in earnest?
MOSCA.   "One
Of ebony——"
CORVINO.   Or do you but delude me?
MOSCA. "The other, mother of pearl"—I am very busy.
Good faith, it is a fortune thrown upon me——
"Item, one salt of agate"—not my seeking.   160
LADY WOULDBE. Do you hear, sir?
MOSCA.   "A perfumed box"—Pray you forbear,
You see I'm troubled—"made of an onyx——"
LADY WOULDBE.   How!
MOSCA. Tomorrow or next day, I shall be at leisure
To talk with you all.
CORVINO.   Is this my large hope's issue?

---

142 **diaper** linen woven in a particular pattern   149 **i' . . .
garters** *i.e.,* with which they may hang themselves   160 **salt**
saltcellar

 LADY WOULDBE. Sir, I must have a fairer answer.
 MOSCA.   Madam!
Marry, and shall: pray you, fairly quit my house.
Nay, raise no tempest with your looks; but hark you,
Remember what your ladyship offered me
To put you in an heir; go to, think on 't;
170 And what you said e'en your best madams did
For maintenance, and why not you? Enough.
Go home, and use the poor Sir Poll, your knight, well,
For fear I tell some riddles. Go, be melancholic.
          [*Exit* LADY WOULDBE.]
 VOLPONE. —O my fine devil!
 CORVINO.   Mosca, pray you a word.
 MOSCA. Lord! Will not you take your dispatch hence yet?
Methinks of all you should have been th' example.
Why should you stay here? With what thought? What
  promise?
Hear you, do not you know I know you an ass,
And that you would most fain have been a wittol
180 If fortune would have let you? That you are
A declared cuckold, on good terms? This pearl,
You'll say, was yours? Right. This diamond?
I'll not deny't, but thank you. Much here else?
It may be so. Why, think that these good works
May help to hide your bad. I'll not betray you;
Although you be but extraordinary,
And have it only in title, it sufficeth.
Go home, be melancholic too, or mad. [*Exit* CORVINO.]
 VOLPONE. —Rare, Mosca! How his villainy becomes him!
190 VOLTORE. Certain, he doth delude all these for me.
 CORBACCIO. Mosca the heir?
 VOLPONE.   O, his four eyes have found it!
 CORBACCIO. I'm cozened, cheated, by a parasite slave!
Harlot, th'ast gulled me.
 MOSCA.   Yes, sir. Stop your mouth,
Or I shall draw the only tooth is left.
Are not you he, that filthy, covetous wretch,
With the three legs, that here, in hope of prey,

168 **Remember . . . heir** Mosca's wording indicates that Lady
Wouldbe has made indecent proposals to him 179 **wittol**
willing cuckold 186 **Although . . . title** Although you are
an unusual cuckold, having only the name 191 **four eyes**
Corbaccio wears spectacles 193 **Harlot** rascal 196 **three legs**
his own and his cane, alluding to the Sphinx's riddle of human
life

Have, any time this three year, snuffed about
With your most grov'ling nose; and would have hired
Me to the pois'ning of my patron, sir?
Are not you he that have today in court   200
Professed the disinheriting of your son?
Perjured yourself? Go home, and die, and stink;
If you but croak a syllable, all comes out.
Away, and call your porters! [*Exit* CORBACCIO.] Go, go,
    stink.
    VOLPONE. —Excellent varlet!
    VOLTORE.   Now, my faithful Mosca,
I find thy constancy——
    MOSCA.   Sir?
    VOLTORE.   Sincere.
    MOSCA.   "A table
Of porphyry"—I mar'l you'll be thus troublesome.
    VOLTORE. Nay, leave off now, they are gone.
    MOSCA.   Why, who are you?
What! Who did send for you? O, cry you mercy,
Reverend sir! Good faith, I am grieved for you,   210
That any chance of mine should thus defeat
Your—I must needs say—most deserving travails.
But I protest, sir, it was cast upon me,
And I could almost wish to be without it,
But that the will o' th' dead must be observed.
Marry, my joy is that you need it not;
You have a gift, sir,—thank your education—
Will never let you want, while there are men
And malice to breed causes. Would I had
But half the like, for all my fortune, sir!   220
If I have any suits,—as I do hope,
Things being so easy and direct, I shall not—
I will make bold with your obstreperous aid,
Conceive me, for your fee, sir. In meantime,
You that have so much law, I know ha' the conscience
Not to be covetous of what is mine.
Good sir, I thank you for my plate; 'twill help
To set up a young man. Good faith, you look
As you were costive; best go home and purge, sir.
                              [*Exit* VOLTORE.]
    VOLPONE. Bid him eat lettuce well! My witty mischief,   230
Let me embrace thee. O that I could now
Transform thee to a Venus—Mosca, go,

207 **mar'l** marvel   212 **travails** labors   219 **causes** lawsuits
229 **costive** constipated   230 **lettuce** *i.e.,* as a laxative

Straight take my habit of *clarissimo,*
And walk the streets; be seen, torment 'em more.
We must pursue as well as plot. Who would
Have lost this feast?
    MOSCA.   I doubt it will lose them.
    VOLPONE. O, my recovery shall recover all.
That I could now but think on some disguise
To meet 'em in, and ask 'em questions;
240 How I would vex 'em still at every turn!
    MOSCA. Sir, I can fit you.
    VOLPONE.   Canst thou?
    MOSCA.   Yes, I know
One o' th' *commendatori,* sir, so like you,
Him will I straight make drunk, and bring you his habit.
    VOLPONE. A rare disguise, and answering thy brain!
O, I will be a sharp disease unto 'em.
    MOSCA. Sir, you must look for curses——
    VOLPONE.   Till they burst;
The fox fares ever best when he is curst.   [*Exeunt.*]

SCENE TWO

[*Sir Politic's lodging*]

[*Enter* PEREGRINE *disguised, and three* MERCATORI.]
PEREGRINE. Am I enough disguised?
1ST MERCATORE.   I warrant you.
PEREGRINE. All my ambition is to fright him only.
2ND MERCATORE. If you could ship him away, 'twere ex-
    cellent.
3RD MERCATORE. To Zant, or to Aleppo!
PEREGRINE.   Yes, and ha' his
Adventures put i' th' book of voyages,
And his gulled story registered for truth!
Well, gentlemen, when I am in a while,
And that you think us warm in our discourse,
Know your approaches.
    1ST MERCATORE.   Trust it to our care.
                            [*Exeunt* MERCATORI.]

[*Enter* WOMAN.]

233 **habit** costume   1 **I . . . you** I assure you   5 **book of
voyages** any of the travel collections then popular   6 **gulled
story** story of his gulling

PEREGRINE. Save you, fair lady! Is Sir Poll within? 10
WOMAN. I do not know, sir.
PEREGRINE.   Pray you say unto him,
Here is a merchant, upon earnest business,
Desires to speak with him.
WOMAN.   I will see, sir.   [*Exit.*]
PEREGRINE.   Pray you.
I see the family is all female here.

[*Re-enter* WOMAN.]

WOMAN. He says, sir, he has weighty affairs of state
That now require him whole; some other time
You may possess him.
PEREGRINE.   Pray you say again,
If those require him whole, these will exact him,
Whereof I bring him tidings. [*Exit* WOMAN.] What might
     be
His grave affair of state now? How to make   20
Bolognian sausages here in Venice, sparing
One o' th' ingredients?

[*Re-enter* WOMAN.]

WOMAN.   Sir, he says he knows
By your word "tidings" that you are no statesman,
And therefore wills you stay.
PEREGRINE.   Sweet, pray you return him,
I have not read so many proclamations,
And studied them for words, as he has done,
But—Here he deigns to come.

[*Enter* SIR POLITIC.]

SIR POLITIC.   Sir, I must crave
Your courteous pardon. There hath chanced today
Unkind disaster 'twixt my lady and me,
And I was penning my apology   30
To give her satisfaction, as you came now.
PEREGRINE. Sir, I am grieved I bring you worse disaster:
The gentleman you met at th' port today,
That told you he was newly arrived——
SIR POLITIC.   Ay, was
A fugitive punk?
PEREGRINE.   No, sir, a spy set on you;
And he has made relation to the Senate

23 **"tidings"** a statesman would use the word "intelligence" 34
punk tart

That you professed to him to have a plot
To sell the state of Venice to the Turk.

 Sir Politic. O me!

 Peregrine.   For which warrants are signed by this
  time,

40 To apprehend you, and to search your study
For papers——

 Sir Politic. Alas, sir, I have none but notes
Drawn out of play-books——

 Peregrine.   All the better, sir.

 Sir Politic. And some essays. What shall I do?

 Peregrine.   Sir, best
Convey yourself into a sugar-chest,
Or, if you could lie round, a frail were rare;
And I could send you aboard.

 Sir Politic.   Sir, I but talked so,
For discourse sake merely.   (*They knock without.*)

 Peregrine.   Hark! They are there.

 Sir Politic. I am a wretch, a wretch!

 Peregrine.   What will you do, sir?
Ha' you ne'er a currant-butt to leap into?

50 They'll put you to the rack; you must be sudden.

 Sir Politic. Sir, I have an engine——

 3rd Merchant.   Sir Politic Wouldbe!

 2nd Merchant. Where is he?

 Sir Politic.   That I have thought upon beforetime.

 Peregrine. What is it?

 Sir Politic.   I shall ne'er endure the torture!——
Marry, it is, sir, of a tortoise-shell,
Fitted for these extremities. Pray you, sir, help me.
Here I've a place, sir, to put back my legs;
Please you to lay it on, sir. With this cap,
And my black gloves, I'll lie, sir, like a tortoise,
Till they are gone.

 Peregrine.   And call you this an engine?

60 Sir Politic. Mine own device——Good sir, bid my
  wife's women
To burn my papers.

     (*The three* Mercatori *rush in.*)

 1st Mercatore. Where's he hid?

 3rd Mercatore.   We must,
And will sure find him.

37 **plot . . . Turk** cf. IV.i.130 45 **frail** rush basket for packing
figs 49 **currant-butt** cask for currants 51 **engine** contrivance

2ND MERCATORE.   Which is his study?
1ST MERCATORE.   What
Are you, sir?
PEREGRINE. I'm a merchant, that came here
To look upon this tortoise.
3RD MERCATORE.   How!
1ST MERCATORE.   St. Mark!
What beast is this?
PEREGRINE.   It is a fish.
2ND MERCATORE.   Come out here!
PEREGRINE. Nay, you may strike him, sir, and tread upon
    him.
He'll bear a cart.
1ST MERCATORE. What, to run over him?
PEREGRINE.   Yes.
3RD MERCATORE. Let's jump upon him.
2ND MERCATORE.   Can he not go?
PEREGRINE.   He creeps, sir.
1ST MERCATORE. Let's see him creep.
PEREGRINE.   No, good sir, you will hurt him.
2ND MERCATORE. Heart, I'll see him creep, or prick his 70
    guts!
3RD MERCATORE. Come out here!
PEREGRINE. Pray you, sir.   [*Aside to* SIR POLITIC.]
    —Creep a little.
1ST MERCATORE.   Forth.
2ND MERCATORE. Yet further.
PEREGRINE.   Good sir!—Creep.
2ND MERCATORE.   We'll see his legs.
    (*They pull off the shell and discover* SIR POLITIC.)
3RD MERCATORE. God's so', he has garters!
1ST MERCATORE.   Ay, and gloves!
2ND MERCATORE.   Is this
Your fearful tortoise?
PEREGRINE.   Now, Sir Poll, we are even;
For your next project I shall be prepared.
I am sorry for the funeral of your notes, sir.
    1ST MERCATORE. 'Twere a rare motion to be seen in
    Fleet Street.
    2ND MERCATORE. Ay, i' the term.
    1ST MERCATORE.   Or Smithfield, in the fair.
    3RD MERCATORE. Methinks 'tis but a melancholic sight.
68 **go** walk   77 **motion** puppet show   **Fleet Street** where freaks
were exhibited   78 **term** the academic term of the law courts,
when country visitors flocked to London   **Smithfield . . . fair**
Bartholomew Fair, where sideshows abounded

PEREGRINE. Farewell, most politic tortoise!

                [*Exeunt* PEREGRINE *and* MERCATORI.]

80   SIR POLITIC.   Where's my lady?

Knows she of this?

    WOMAN.   I know not, sir.

    SIR POLITIC.   Inquire. [*Exit* WOMAN.]

—O, I shall be the fable of all feasts,

The freight of the *gazetti*, ship-boys' tale,

And, which is worst, even talk for ordinaries.

                [*Re-enter* WOMAN.]

    WOMAN. My lady's come most melancholic home,

And says, sir, she will straight to sea, for physic.

    SIR POLITIC. And I, to shun this place and clime forever,

Creeping with house on back, and think it well

To shrink my poor head in my politic shell.   [*Exeunt.*]

SCENE THREE

[*Volpone's house*]

(*Enter* VOLPONE *in the habit of a commendatore, and*
      MOSCA *in that of a clarissimo.*)

    VOLPONE. Am I then like him?

    MOSCA.   O sir, you are he;

No man can sever you.

    VOLPONE.   Good.

    MOSCA.   But what am I?

    VOLPONE. 'Fore heav'n, a brave *clarissimo*, thou becom'st
    it!

Pity thou wert not born one.

    MOSCA. [*Aside.*]   —If I hold

My made one, 'twill be well.

    VOLPONE.   I'll go and see

What news first at the court.   [*Exit.*]

    MOSCA.   Do so.—My fox

Is out on his hole, and ere he shall re-enter,

I'll make him languish in his borrowed case,

Except he come to composition with me.—

Androgyno, Castrone, Nano!

    [*Enter* ANDROGYNO, CASTRONE, *and* NANO.]

10   ALL.   Here.

83 **freight . . . gazetti** subject of newspaper reports 7 **on** of
8 **case** disguise 9 **Except . . . me** unless he makes a deal with
me

Mosca. Go, recreate yourselves abroad; go, sport.

[*Exeunt.*]

So, now I have the keys, and am possessed.
Since he will needs be dead afore his time,
I'll bury him or gain by him. I'm his heir,
And so will keep me, till he share at least.
To cozen him of all were but a cheat
Well placed; no man would construe it a sin.
Let his sport pay for 't. This is called the fox-trap.

[*Exit.*]

Scene Four

[A *street*]

[*Enter* Corbaccio *and* Corvino.]

Corbaccio. They say the court is set.

Corvino.   We must maintain
Our first tale good, for both our reputations.

Corbaccio. Why, mine's no tale! My son would there
    have killed me.

Corvino. That's true, I had forgot. [*Aside.*] —Mine is,
    I'm sure.—
But for your will, sir.

Corbaccio.   Ay, I'll come upon him
For that hereafter, now his patron's dead.

[*Enter* Volpone.]

Volpone. Signor Corvino! And Corbaccio! Sir,
Much joy unto you.

Corvino.   Of what?

Volpone.   The sudden good
Dropped down upon you——

Corbaccio.   Where?

Volpone.   And none knows how,
From old Volpone, sir.

Corbaccio.   Out, arrant knave!   10

Volpone. Let not your too much wealth, sir, make you
    furious.

Corbaccio. Away, thou varlet.

Volpone.   Why, sir?

12 **varlet** sergeant. Volpone is dressed as an officer of the court.

CORBACCIO.   Dost thou mock me?
VOLPONE. You mock the world, sir; did you not change
    wills?
CORBACCIO. Out, harlot!
VOLPONE.   O! Belike you are the man,
Signor Corvino? Faith, you carry it well;
You grow not mad withal. I love your spirit.
You are not over-leavened with your fortune.
You should ha' some would swell now, like a wine-vat,
With such an autumn—Did he gi' you all, sir?
    CORVINO. Avoid, you rascal.
20   VOLPONE.   Troth, your wife has shown
Herself a very woman! But you are well,
You need not care; you have a good estate,
To bear it out, sir, better by this chance—
Except Corbaccio have a share.
    CORBACCIO.   Hence, varlet.
VOLPONE. You will not be a'known, sir? Why, 'tis wise.
Thus do all gamesters, at all games, dissemble.
No man will seem to win. [Exeunt CORVINO and CORBAC-
    CIO.] Here comes my vulture,
Heaving his beak up i' the air, and snuffing.

[Enter VOLTORE.]

    VOLTORE. Outstripped thus, by a parasite! A slave,
30 Would run on errands, and make legs for crumbs!
Well, what I'll do——
    VOLPONE.   The court stays for your worship.
I e'en rejoice, sir, at your worship's happiness,
And that it fell into so learnèd hands,
That understand the fingering——
    VOLTORE.   What do you mean?
VOLPONE. I mean to be a suitor to your worship,
For the small tenement, out of reparations,
That at the end of your long row of houses,
By the Peschería—it was, in Volpone's time,
Your predecessor, ere he grew diseased,
40 A handsome, pretty, customed bawdy-house
As any was in Venice, none dispraised;
But fell with him. His body and that house
Decayed together.

14 belike perhaps 20 Avoid Begone 21 very true 25
a'known acknowledged 36 out . . . reparations in disrepair
38 Peschería fish market 40 customed frequented by clients
41 dispraised slighted

VOLTORE.   Come, sir, leave your prating.

VOLPONE. Why, if your worship give me but your hand,
That I may ha' the refusal, I have done.
'Tis a mere toy to you, sir, candle-rents.
As your learned worship knows——

VOLTORE.   What do I know?

VOLPONE. Marry, no end of your wealth, sir, God de-
crease it!

VOLTORE. Mistaking knave! What, mock'st thou my mis-
fortune?   [*Exit.*]

VOLPONE. His blessing on your heart, sir; would 'twere 50
more!

Now to my first again, at the next corner.

[*Enter* CORBACCIO *and* CORVINO, MOSCA *passing over the
stage.*]

CORBACCIO. See, in our habit! See the impudent varlet!

CORVINO. That I could shoot mine eyes at him, like gun-
stones!

VOLPONE. But is this true, sir, of the parasite?

CORBACCIO. Again, t' afflict us? Monster!

VOLPONE.   In good faith, sir,
I'm heartily grieved, a beard of your grave length
Should be so over-reached. I never brooked
That parasite's hair; methought his nose should cozen.
There still was somewhat in his look, did promise
The bane of a *clarissimo*.

CORBACCIO.   Knave——

VOLPONE.   Methinks   60
Yet you, that are so traded i' the world,
A witty merchant, the fine bird, Corvino,
That have such moral emblems on your name,
Should not have sung your shame; and dropped your
cheese,
To let the fox laugh at your emptiness.

CORVINO. Sirrah, you think the privilege of the place,
And your red saucy cap, that seems to me

44 **hand** signature   46 **candle-rents** income from deteriorating
property   53 **gun-stones** stone cannonballs   57 **over-reached**
outwitted   59 **still** always   **somewhat** something   63 **moral
emblems** emblem books conveyed moral lessons by means of
engravings, or emblems, in which animals like the crow were
used to represent human vices   64 **sung . . . emptiness** Aesop's
fable of the fox and the crow, a typical subject for an emblem

Nailed to your jolt-head with those two chequìns,
Can warrant your abuses. Come you hither.
70 You shall perceive, sir, I dare beat you. Approach.
    VOLPONE. No haste, sir, I do know your valor well,
Since you durst publish what you are, sir.
    CORVINO.   Tarry,
I'd speak with you.
    VOLPONE.   Sir, sir, another time——
    CORVINO. Nay, now.
    VOLPONE.   O God, sir! I were a wise man,
Would stand the fury of a distracted cuckold.

                       (MOSCA *walks by them.*)
    CORBACCIO. What, come again!
    VOLPONE.   —Upon 'em, Mosca; save me.
    CORBACCIO. The air's infected where he breathes.
    CORVINO.   Let's fly him.
             [*Exeunt* CORVINO *and* CORBACCIO.]
    VOLPONE. Excellent basilisk! Turn upon the vulture.

             [*Enter* VOLTORE.]

    VOLTORE. Well, flesh-fly, it is summer with you now;
Your winter will come on.
80   MOSCA.   Good advocate,
Pray thee not rail, nor threaten out of place thus;
Thou'lt make a solecism, as Madam says.
Get you a biggen more; your brain breaks loose.   [*Exit.*]
    VOLTORE. Well, sir.
    VOLPONE.   Would you ha' me beat the insolent
      slave?
Throw dirt upon his first good clothes?
    VOLTORE.   —This same
Is doubtless some familiar!
    VOLPONE.   Sir, the court,
In troth, stays for you. I am mad, a mule
That never read Justinian, should get up
And ride an advocate. Had you no quirk
90 To avoid gullage, sir, by such a creature?
I hope you do but jest; he has not done 't;

68 **jolt-head** blockhead **two chequìns** two gilt buttons on a
commendatore's cap   78 **basilisk** fabulous serpent whose mere
look was fatal   83 **biggen** skull-cap worn by lawyers   86
familiar attendant devil   88 **Justinian** the compilation of Roman
law made under the sixth-century Byzantine Emperor Justinian
89 **quirk** trick

This's but confederacy to blind the rest.
You are the heir?
    VOLTORE.   A strange, officious,
Troublesome knave! Thou dost torment me.
    VOLPONE.   I know——
It cannot be, sir, that you should be cozened;
'Tis not within the wit of man to do it.
You are so wise, so prudent; and 'tis fit
That wealth and wisdom still should go together.
                                  [Exeunt.]

SCENE FIVE

[*The Scrutineo*]

[*Enter four* AVOCATORI, NOTARIO, BONARIO, CELIA, COR-
BACCIO, CORVINO, COMMENDATORI, *&c.*]

    1ST AVOCATORE. Are all the parties here?
    NOTARIO.   All but the advocate.
    2ND AVOCATORE. And here he comes.

[*Enter* VOLTORE *and* VOLPONE.]

    1ST AVOCATORE. Then bring 'em forth to sentence.
    VOLTORE. O my most honored fathers, let your mercy
Once win upon your justice, to forgive—
I am distracted——
    VOLPONE. [*Aside.*] —What will he do now?
    VOLTORE.   O,
I know not which t' address myself to first;
Whether your fatherhoods, or these innocents——
    CORVINO. [*Aside.*] —Will he betray himself?
    VOLTORE.   Whom equally
I have abused, out of most covetous ends——
    CORVINO. The man is mad!
    CORBACCIO.   What's that?
    CORVINO.   He is possessed. 10
    VOLTORE. For which, now struck in conscience, here I
      prostrate
Myself at your offended feet, for pardon.
    1ST, 2ND AVOCATORI. Arise.
    CELIA.   O heav'n, how just thou art!
    VOLPONE. [*Aside.*]   —I'm caught
I' mine own noose——

10 **possessed** *i.e.*, by a devil

CORVINO. [*Aside to* CORBACCIO.] —Be constant, sir;
  nought now
Can help but impudence.
    1ST AVOCATORE.   Speak forward.
    COMMENDATORE.   Silence!
    VOLTORE. It is not passion in me, reverend fathers,
But only conscience, conscience, my good sires,
That makes me now tell truth. That parasite,
That knave, hath been the instrument of all.
    1ST AVOCATORE. Where is that knave? Fetch him.
    VOLPONE.   I go.   [*Exit.*]
20   CORVINO.   Grave fathers,
This man's distracted; he confessed it now.
For, hoping to be old Volpone's heir,
Who now is dead——
    3RD AVOCATORE.   How!
    2ND AVOCATORE.   Is Volpone dead?
    CORVINO. Dead since, grave fathers.—
    BONARIO.   O sure vengeance!
    1ST AVOCATORE.   Stay,
Then he was no deceiver.
    VOLTORE.   O, no, none;
The parasite, grave fathers.
    CORVINO.   He does speak
Out of mere envy, 'cause the servant's made
The thing he gaped for. Please your fatherhoods,
This is the truth; though I'll not justify
30 The other, but he may be some-deal faulty.
    VOLTORE. Ay, to your hopes, as well as mine, Corvino.
But I'll use modesty. Pleaseth your wisdoms
To view these certain notes, and but confer them;
As I hope favor, they shall speak clear truth.
    CORVINO. The devil has entered him!
    BONARIO.   Or bides in you.
    4TH AVOCATORE. We have done ill, by a public officer
To send for him, if he be heir.
    2ND AVOCATORE.   For whom?
    4TH AVOCATORE. Him that they call the parasite.
    3RD AVOCATORE.   'Tis true,
He is a man of great estate now left.
40   4TH AVOCATORE. —Go you, and learn his name, and say
  the court
Entreats his presence here, but to the clearing
Of some few doubts.   [*Exit* NOTARIO.]

33 **certain** particular **confer** compare

2ND AVOCATORE. This same's a labyrinth!

1ST AVOCATORE. Stand you unto your first report?

CORVINO.   My state,
My life, my fame——

BONARIO.   Where is't?

CORVINO.   Are at the stake.

1ST AVOCATORE. Is yours so too?

CORBACCIO.   The advocate's a knave,
And has a forkèd tongue——

2ND AVOCATORE.   Speak to the point.

CORBACCIO. So is the parasite too.

1ST AVOCATORE.   This is confusion.

VOLTORE. I do beseech your fatherhoods, read but
those—

CORVINO. And credit nothing the false spirit hath writ.
It cannot be but he is possessed, grave fathers.   50

[*The scene closes.*]

SCENE SIX

[*A street*]

[*Enter* VOLPONE.]

VOLPONE. To make a snare for mine own neck! And run
My head into it wilfully, with laughter!
When I had newly 'scaped, was free and clear!
Out of mere wantonness! O, the dull devil
Was in this brain of mine when I devised it,
And Mosca gave it second; he must now
Help to sear up this vein, or we bleed dead.

[*Enter* NANO, ANDROGYNO, *and* CASTRONE.]

How now! Who let you loose? Whither go you now?
What, to buy gingerbread, or to drown kitlings?

NANO. Sir, Master Mosca called us out of doors,   10
And bid us all go play, and took the keys.

ANDROGYNO.   Yes.

VOLPONE. Did Master Mosca take the keys? Why, so!
I am farther in. These are my fine conceits!
I must be merry, with a mischief to me!
What a vile wretch was I, that could not bear

9 **kitlings** kittens   13 **conceits** notions

My fortune soberly. I must ha' my crotchets
And my conundrums!—Well, go you and seek him.—
His meaning may be truer than my fear.—
Bid him, he straight come to me to the court;
20 Thither will I, and, if't be possible,
Unscrew my advocate, upon new hopes.
When I provoked him, then I lost myself.   [*Exeunt.*]

Scene Seven

[*The Scrutineo*]

[*Four* Avocatori, Notario, Voltore, Bonario, Celia,
Corbaccio, Corvino, &c., *as before.*]

1st Avocatore. These things can ne'er be reconciled.
        He here
Professeth that the gentleman was wronged,
And that the gentlewoman was brought thither,
Forced by her husband, and there left.
        Voltore.   Most true.
        Celia. How ready is heav'n to those that pray!
        1st Avocatore.   But that
Volpone would have ravished her, he holds
Utterly false, knowing his impotence.
        Corvino. Grave fathers, he is possessed; again, I say,
Possessed. Nay, if there be possession and
Obsession, he has both.
10   3rd Avocatore.   Here comes our officer.

[*Enter* Volpone.]

Volpone. The parasite will straight be here, grave fa-
        thers.
        4th Avocatore. You might invent some other name, sir
        varlet.
        3rd Avocatore. Did not the notary meet him?
        Voltore.   Not that I know.
        4th Avocatore. His coming will clear all.
        2nd Avocatore.   Yet it is misty.
        Voltore. May't please your fatherhoods——
        Volpone. (*Whispers to* Voltore.) Sir, the parasite
Willed me to tell you that his master lives;

18 His . . . fear His intentions may be more loyal than I suspect   8 possession the evil spirit within the body   9 obsession
the evil spirit attacking from without

That you are still the man; your hopes the same;
And this was only a jest——
 VOLTORE.   How?
 VOLPONE.   Sir, to try
If you were firm, and how you stood affected.
 VOLTORE. Art sure he lives?
 VOLPONE.   Do I live, sir?
 VOLTORE.   O me!   20
I was too violent.
 VOLPONE. Sir, you may redeem it:
They said you were possessed; fall down, and seem so.
I'll help to make it good. (VOLTORE *falls.*) God bless the
 man!— [*Aside to* VOLTORE.]
Stop your wind hard, and swell—See, see, see, see!
He vomits crooked pins! His eyes are set,
Like a dead hare's hung in a poulter's shop!
His mouth's running away! Do you see, signor?
Now 'tis in his belly.
 CORVINO.   —Ay, the devil!
 VOLPONE. Now in his throat.
 CORVINO.   —Ay, I perceive it plain.
 VOLTORE. 'Twill out, 'twill out! Stand clear. See where it 30
 flies,
In shape of a blue toad, with a bat's wings!
Do not you see it, sir?
 CORBACCIO. What? I think I do.
 CORVINO. —'Tis too manifest.
 VOLPONE.   Look! He comes t' himself!
 VOLTORE. Where am I?
 VOLPONE. Take good heart, the worst is past, sir.
You are dispossessed.
 1ST AVOCATORE. What accident is this?
 2ND AVOCATORE. Sudden, and full of wonder!
 3RD AVOCATORE.   If he were
Possessed, as it appears, all this is nothing.
 CORVINO. He has been often subject to these fits.
 1ST AVOCATORE. Show him that writing.—Do you know
 it, sir?
 VOLPONE. [*Aside to* VOLTORE.] —Deny it, sir, forswear 40
 it, know it not.
 VOLTORE. Yes, I do know it well, it is my hand;
But all that it contains is false.

25 **vomits . . . belly** Voltore's symptoms are taken from con-
temporary accounts of witchcraft 26 **poulter** seller of poultry
and game 27 **running away** distorted

BONARIO.   O practice!
2ND AVOCATORE. What maze is this!
1ST AVOCATORE.   Is he not guilty then,
Whom you there name the parasite?
VOLTORE.   Grave fathers,
No more than his good patron, old Volpone.
4TH AVOCATORE. Why, he is dead.
VOLTORE.   O, no, my honored fathers,
He lives——
1ST AVOCATORE. How! Lives?
VOLTORE.   Lives.
2ND AVOCATORE.   This is subtler yet!
3RD AVOCATORE. You said he was dead.
VOLTORE.   Never.
3RD AVOCATORE.   You said so!
CORVINO.   I heard so.
4TH AVOCATORE. Here comes the gentleman; make him
    way.
3RD AVOCATORE. A stool!   [Enter MOSCA.]
50 4TH AVOCATORE. [Aside.] —A proper man and, were
    Volpone dead,
A fit match for my daughter.
3RD AVOCATORE.   Give him way.
VOLPONE. [Aside to MOSCA.] —Mosca, I was almost lost;
    the advocate
Had betrayed all; but now it is recovered.
All's o' the hinge again——Say I am living.
MOSCA. What busy knave is this?—Most reverend fa-
    thers,
I sooner had attended your grave pleasures,
But that my order for the funeral
Of my dear patron did require me——
VOLPONE. [Aside.]   —Mosca!
MOSCA. Whom I intend to bury like a gentleman.
VOLPONE. [Aside.] —Ay, quick, and cozen me of all.
60 2ND AVOCATORE.   Still stranger!
More intricate!
1ST AVOCATORE. And come about again!
4TH AVOCATORE. [Aside.] —It is a match, my daughter
    is bestowed.
MOSCA. [Aside to VOLPONE.] —Will you gi' me half?
VOLPONE.   First I'll be hanged.
MOSCA.   I know

50 **proper** handsome   55 **busy** meddlesome   59 **quick** alive

Your voice is good, cry not so loud.

1ST AVOCATORE.   Demand
The advocate.—Sir, did not you affirm
Volpone was alive?

VOLPONE.   Yes, and he is;
This gent'man told me so. [*Aside to* MOSCA.] —Thou shalt
    have half.

MOSCA. Whose drunkard is this same? Speak, some that
    know him.
I never saw his face. [*Aside to* VOLPONE.] —I cannot now
Afford it you so cheap.

VOLPONE.   No?

1ST AVOCATORE.   What say you?   70

VOLTORE. The officer told me.

VOLPONE.   I did, grave fathers,
And will maintain he lives, with mine own life,
And that this creature told me. [*Aside.*] —I was born
With all good stars my enemies!

MOSCA.   Most grave fathers,
If such an insolence as this must pass
Upon me, I am silent; 'twas not this
For which you sent, I hope.

2ND AVOCATORE.   Take him away.

VOLPONE. —Mosca!

3RD AVOCATORE.   Let him be whipped.

VOLPONE.   —Wilt thou betray me?
Cozen me?

3RD AVOCATORE. And taught to bear himself
Toward a person of his rank.

4TH AVOCATORE. [*The officers seize* VOLPONE.] Away. 80

MOSCA. I humbly thank your fatherhoods.

VOLPONE.   —Soft, soft. Whipped!
And lose all that I have! If I confess,
It cannot be much more.

4TH AVOCATORE.   Sir, are you married?

VOLPONE. —They'll be allied anon; I must be resolute:
The fox shall here uncase.   (*Puts off his disguise.*)

MOSCA.   Patron!

VOLPONE.   Nay, now
My ruins shall not come alone; your match
I'll hinder sure: my substance shall not glue you
Nor screw you into a family.

MOSCA.   Why, patron!

VOLPONE. I am Volpone, and this is my knave;

64 Demand Question

90 This, his own knave; this, avarice's fool;
This, a chimera of wittol, fool, and knave.
And, reverend fathers, since we all can hope
Nought but a sentence, let's not now despair it.
You hear me brief.

    CORVINO.   May it please your fatherhoods——
    COMMENDATORE.   Silence!
    1ST AVOCATORE. The knot is now undone by miracle.
    2ND AVOCATORE. Nothing can be more clear.
    3RD AVOCATORE.   Or can more prove
These innocent.
    1ST AVOCATORE. Give 'em their liberty.
    BONARIO. Heaven could not long let such gross crimes be
      hid.
    2ND AVOCATORE. If this be held the highway to get
      riches,
May I be poor!

100   3RD AVOCATORE. This's not the gain, but torment.
    1ST AVOCATORE. These possess wealth, as sick men pos-
      sess fevers,
Which trulier may be said to possess them.
    2ND AVOCATORE. Disrobe that parasite.
    CORVINO, MOSCA.   Most honored fathers——
    1ST AVOCATORE. Can you plead aught to stay the course
      of justice?
If you can, speak.
    CORVINO, VOLTORE. We beg favor.
    CELIA.   And mercy.
    1ST AVOCATORE. You hurt your innocence, suing for the
      guilty.——
Stand forth; and first the parasite.—You appear
T'have been the chiefest minister, if not plotter,
In all these lewd impostures; and now, lastly,
110 Have with your impudence abused the court
And habit of a gentleman of Venice,
Being a fellow of no birth or blood;
For which our sentence is, first thou be whipped;
Then live perpetual prisoner in our galleys.
    VOLPONE. I thank you for him.
    MOSCA.   Bane to thy wolfish nature!
    1ST AVOCATORE. Deliver him to the *Saffi*. [MOSCA *is car-*
      ried out.] —Thou, Volpone,
By blood and rank a gentleman, canst not fall

90-91 **This . . . this . . . this** pointing in turn to Voltore,
Corbaccio, and Corvino   91 **chimera** fabulous monster, a com-
posite of lion, goat, and serpent

Under like censure; but our judgment on thee
Is that thy substance all be straight confiscate
To the hospital of the *Incurabili*.   120
And since the most was gotten by imposture,
By feigning lame, gout, palsy, and such diseases,
Thou art to lie in prison, cramped with irons,
Till thou be'st sick and lame indeed.—Remove him.

    VOLPONE. This is called mortifying of a fox.

    1ST AVOCATORE. Thou, Voltore, to take away the scandal
Thou hast giv'n all worthy men of thy profession,
Art banished from their fellowship, and our state.—
Corbaccio, bring him near!—We here possess
Thy son of all thy state, and confine thee   130
To the monastery of San Spirito;
Where, since thou knew'st not how to live well here,
Thou shalt be learned to die well.

    CORBACCIO.   Ha! What said he?

    COMMENDATORE. You shall know anon, sir.

    1ST AVOCATORE.   Thou, Corvino, shalt
Be straight embarked from thine own house, and rowed
Round about Venice, through the Grand Canal,
Wearing a cap, with fair long ass's ears
Instead of horns; and so to mount, a paper
Pinned on thy breast, to the *Berlina*—

    CORVINO.   Yes,
And have mine eyes beat out with stinking fish,   140
Bruised fruit, and rotten eggs—'Tis well. I'm glad
I shall not see my shame yet.

    1ST AVOCATORE.   And to expiate
Thy wrongs done to thy wife, thou art to send her
Home to her father, with her dowry trebled.
And these are all your judgments——

    ALL.   Honored fathers!

    1ST AVOCATORE. Which may not be revoked. Now you
      begin,
When crimes are done and past, and to be punished,
To think what your crimes are.—Away with them!
Let all that see these vices thus rewarded,
Take heart, and love to study 'em. Mischiefs feed   150
Like beasts, till they be fat, and then they bleed.

                              [Exeunt.]

[VOLPONE *comes forward.*]

119 **substance** property   120 **Incurabili** incurables   125 **morti-
fying** chastening. To mortify fowl was to hang it until tender
enough for cooking.

VOLPONE. The seasoning of a play is the applause.
Now, though the fox be punished by the laws,
He yet doth hope there is no suff'ring due,
For any fact which he hath done 'gainst you.
If there be, censure him; here he doubtful stands.
If not, fare jovially, and clap your hands.   [*Exit.*]

155 **fact** crime

BIBLIOGRAPHY

EDITIONS

Herford, C. H., and Simpson, Percy and Evelyn, eds. *Ben Jonson*, 11 vols. (Oxford, 1925-52).

Levin, Harry, ed. *Ben Jonson: Selected Works* (New York, 1938).

Rea, John D., ed. *Volpone*, Yale Studies in English (New Haven, 1919).

CRITICISM

Swinburne, Algernon Charles, *A Study of Ben Jonson* (London, 1889).

Simpson, Percy, "The Masque," in *Shakespeare's England* (Oxford, 1916), II, 311-333.

Herford and Simpson, vols. I and II, *The Man and his Work* (see above).

Eliot, T. S., "Ben Jonson," in *Elizabethan Essays* (London, 1934).

Knights, L. C., *Drama and Society in the Age of Jonson* (New York, 1937).

Levin, Harry, "Jonson's Metempsychosis," *Philological Quarterly*, XXII (1943), 231-239.

Barish, Jonas A., "The Double Plot in *Volpone*," *Modern Philology*, LI (1953), 83-92.

Hays, H. R., "Satire and Identification: An Introduction to Ben Jonson," *Kenyon Review*, XIX (1957), 267-283.

Enck, John J., *Jonson and the Comic Truth* (Madison, Wisconsin, 1957).

111